TEACHING
OF
SCIENCE

Edited by
M.S. Yadav

ANMOL PUBLICATIONS PVT. LTD.
NEW DELHI - 110 002 (INDIA)

ANMOL PUBLICATIONS PVT. LTD.
H.O.: 4374/4B, Ansari Road, Darya Ganj
New Delhi-110 002 (India)
Ph.: 23278000, 23261597
B.O.: 1015, Ist Main Road, BSK IIIrd Stage
IIIrd Phase, IIIrd Block
Bangalore - 560 085 (Karnataka)
Ph: 080-517 3429, Tel/Fax: 080-2672 3604
Visit us at: www.anmolpublications.com

Teaching of Science

First Edition, 1992

Reprint, 1995, 1996, 1997, 2000, 2002, 2003, 2004, 2005

Reprint, 2007 , 2009

PRINTED IN INDIA

Printed at Mehra Offset Press, Delhi.

Preface

This book titled "Teaching of Science" has been written to help the students in understanding the aims, objectives, techniques and methods used for teaching of science in schools. Though the book is of general nature but an effort has been made to cover up most of the topics prescribed for 'Teaching of Science' paper in B.Ed. classes of the Indian Universities. Emphasis has been placed to discuss all such topics keeping Indian conditions in view. A comparative study of the place of science in schools in various countries has been included to emphasise the importance being attached to teaching of science at present. To illustrate a point and for various other illustrations and explanations the material from reports of various education commissions appointed by Government of India (Kothari Commission) and UNESCO's international commission and recommendations of many other committees (e.g. Tara Devi Seminar Report, NCERT Recommendations) have been included at appropriate places.

The author is indebted to many authors whose works have been frequently consulted while preparing the book and expresses his gratitude to all such persons.

Author would also like to express his sincere gratitude to a number of friends and collegues who gave many invaluable suggestions for improvement of the book. I am also thankful to my publishers M/s Anmol Publications for bringing out the book in such a good shape and such a short time.

Author earnestly hopes that the book will be liked by students and teachers alike. Comments and suggestions for the further improvement of the book will be gratefully accepted.

Author

Contents

CHAPTER 1

Introduction

1.1 WHAT IS SCIENCE?

Man has been trying to understand the changes going around him and has been constantly receiving a great number of impressions through his various senses such as hearing, sight, smell, taste and touch. Making an effective use of his senses and using his communicative ability he *accumulated information* about his surroundings, *organised this information* and sought regularities in it and tried to find out *why the regularities exist* and finally transmitted his findings to the next generation.

This systematised store of human knowledge gained after generalising and interrelating the various isolated fucts in known as science.

The word science has its origin from a Latin word 'Scientia' meaning 'to know'. Science in universal but has been defined in different ways, e.g.

"Science is a systematised body of knowledge."

"Science is nothing but organised common sense."

"Science is a heap of truth."

John Woodburn and **E.O. Obourn** consider *science as that human endeavour that seeks to describe with even increasing accuracy, the events and circumstances which occur or exist within our natural environment.*

The definition of science found in **report on Policies for Science Education** is *'Science is a cumulative and endless series of empirical observations which result in the formation of concepts and theories, with both concepts and theories being subject to modification in light of further empirical observations. Science in both a body of knowledge and the process of acquiring and refining knowledge.*

Thus science is simultaneously a *body of knowledge* and *continuous, self evaluative process of enquiry.*

Science thus has two important approaches

(*a*) Science as a Product.

(*b*) Science as a Process.

Various laws, theories, principles etc. are included in the category of *science as a product* where as scientific attitude, scientific method etc. form part of *science as a process* though both aspects are important in their own way but to attain the aims of science education in schools more emphasis will be placed on process approach.

1.2 IMPACT OF SCIENCE AND TECHNOLOGY

Impact of Science on Modern Living

Science has revolutionised our life style and also brought about tremendous changes in our way of thinking, attitudes, outlook etc. The effect of science is visible all around us. Science has brought about a change in such important aspects as health, communication, transportation, power etc. It can now be said without any hesitation that we owe our very existence to science the average span of human life has been doubled.

Just as science is universal so also its benefits are universal. Its material benefits are immence and have far reaching effects. The important of these are *industrialization of agriculture* and *release of nuclear energy.* In addition to its contribution to material benefits science has also contributed a lot to the culture. Actually speaking modern world has been created by science and is being maintained by science.

These effects of science can be summarised as follows:

(*a*) *Impact of Science in Agriculture.* "Green Revolution" was possible only because of science. Science mechanised agriculture and 'green revolution' was possible only because of such a mechanised farming. By mechanised farming and making use of tools invented by science we can now carry out various agricultural work such as ploughing, sowing, reaping, harvesting etc. quickly and expediously use of fertilizers makes the lands fertile and it increases the yield of crops. The increase in yields of various agricultural products has been made possible by use of scientific techniques for saving the destruction of crops by harmful insects. For prevention of crops from such insects we make use of pesticides and insecticides discovered by scientists. A spray of these insecticides at a proper time helps to increase the crop yield. Presently nuclear energy is also used for obtaining high yields of some commercial crops.

(*b*) *Impact of Science on Health.* Science has contributed a lot in the maintenance and improvement of our health. It helps us in diagnosis, treatment, prevention of various diseases. It is only due to science that we have prevented the human society of contagious diseases and epidemics. For this we make use of various preventive techniques such as vaccination, inoculation, surgical operations etc. We have become health conscious because science has provided us guidance in the fields of hygiene and sanitation, diet, physical exercises etc.

(*c*) *Impact of Science on Industry.* Modern industries depends to a large extent on the discoveries of science. Such discoveries had brought about drastic changes in the ways and processes of industry. The progress in science has made the difficult tasks easier by use of machines. In industrially advanced countries the different tasks are performed by machines and human beings are required only to operate machines. Automatic machines carry out various tasks such as yarn production, weaving and giving a finish etc. in textile industry. Science has brought about major revolutions in various industries including printing industry, radio and television industry, pharmaceuticals, agriculture, armament industry etc.

(*d*) *Impact of Science on Modern Civilization.* Modern civilization owes its existence to science and can be easily called scientific civilization. Various advances in fields of agriculture, medicines, cosmetics, transport, communication etc. have affected our way of living and the modern civilization is due to the effect of such changes in our behaviour. Science has helped us to overcome the age old taboos of superstitions and we find that a large number of unfounded beliefs have faded away. Science has also contributed a lot in the removal of illiteracy and ignorance. It has also brought about a change in our attitude towards religion, marriage, birth control etc.

(*e*) *Impact of Science on Democracy.* It is the change in our attitude which has been brought about by science that we have developed the qualities of a good citizen for democracy. Science helps us to develop an outlook for receiving new ideas and to have a capacity for clear thinking. Science also develops in us a zeal to work for the service of mankind and also to respect the views of others. It also develops our intellectual integrity. These are the very qualities which are expected from an individual. The knowledge of science helps an individual to find useful methods for checking the bias. These ideas developed in an individual are the very basic foundations of democracy.

1.3 PLACE OF SCIENCE IN SCHOOL CURRICULUM

Science is considered as an important subject in school curriculum because the man's future depends to a large extent on scientific advances and development of productive activity. There is great feeling to teach science.

The International Congress on Science and Technology Education convened by Unesco in 1981 made numerous recommendations for Unesco's future role in this broad field of activity.

With the funds provided by Unesco studies were carried out regarding the place of science in curriculum in various countries. Following generalisations were made.

Africa

The data was provided by 21 countries of the region. It was found that in 'primary' classes in most of these countries time was allotted for teaching of Science. The time allotted per week varied from 1 hour to 4.5 hours. Most of the countries adopted integrated approach for teaching of science. In middle classes also science forms a part of the curriculum and in secondary classes general science is a permitted alternative to integrated science. General science includes topics from physics, chemistry and biology only whereas integrated course includes elements of astronomy, geology, agricultural science, home science and economics in addition to physics, chemistry and biology.

Arab States

Ten countries of the region were surveyed. All countries put science firmly on time taste of all grades from 1 to 6. The time allotted per weak for science varies, between 1 to 3.5 hours. At 'intermediate' and secondary level courses in integrated science are provided and for classes 7, 8, 9 generally 2 hours per week are allotted. In grades 10, 11 and 12 these are taught as separate subjects and 2 hours per week is allotted for each subject.

Asia and the Pacific

Seventeen countries of the region including India participated in survey. In almost every country, a course in integrated science is the one most favoured in the early secondary school years. The three traditional science disciplines physics, chemistry and biology, are almost invariably on offer as optional courses during the late secondary school years.

In India through the efforts of National Council of Educational Research and Training (NCERT) science has been made a compulsory subject through out the school stage. In this connection it would be in our interest to consider the views of Kothari Commission and Unesco's international commission on the development of education.

Views of Kothari Commission

Kothari Commission was given the task of suggesting necessary improvements in educational system of the country. It worked during the years 1964-1966 and made a detailed study of educational system in India. It suggested various changes for improvement of education in India. Here we concentrate on the suggestions made by the commission about the science education. The commission suggested that great emphasis be laid on science education and that science be made a compulsory object of the school curriculum. Following lines from the commissions report make the point clear.

"We lay great emphasis on making science an important element in the school curriculum. We therefore, recommend that science and mathematics should be taught on compulsory basis to all pupil as a part of general education during the first ten years of schooling. In addition there should be provision of special course in these subjects at the secondary stage, for students of more than average ability".

Unesco's International Education Commission

The recommendations made by Unesco's International Commission in 1972 are quite similar to those made by Kothari Commission (1964-1966) in India.

The recommendations made by Unesco's International Commission about the teaching of science and technology are as under.

"Science and Technology must become essential components in any educational enterprise; they must be incorporated into all educational activity intended for children, young people and adults, in order to help the individual to control social energies as well as natural and productive ones – thereby achieving mastery over himself, his choices and actions – and finally, they must help man to acquire a scientific turn of mind so that he becomes able to promote science without being enslaved by it".

Furthermore this commission recommended that science be incorporated as a single science. In this respect the recommendation of the commission is as under.

"The natural science will one day incorporate the science of man, just as science of man will incorporate the natural sciences; There will be a *single sciences*".

1.4 VALUES OF SCIENCE IN EVERY DAY LIFE

Present age is known as the age of science and so science is considered an important subject in the school curriculum. In this era of science larger number of people are being employed in scientific pursuits and for this they need a knowledge of science. The dawn of space age and explosion in knowledge have also necessitated the teaching of science to every student.

Science education is essential as it is of immense value in the students' individual life as also his life in society. Science education is important due to the following reasons:

(*a*) Intellectual Value

Science alongwith being a content of knowledge is a method of acquiring knowledge. Scientific knowledge helps to sharpen our intellect and promotes intellectual honesty. It helps us to report about things and events without any bias. It makes us quite systematic in our reasoning. It helps us in acquiring the strength to face hardships and failures because the pursuit of science requires diligence and patience. The science education can develop the positive attitudes like open mindedness, reasoning etc. Such a positive attitude is quite helpful to an individual to understand , evaluate and solve many a social problems be faces in life and helps him to lead a happy, successful and satisfying life.

(*b*) Vocational Value

In the present age we do not find any vocation that does not need the knowledge of science more ever there are a large number of vocations for which study by science is a primary requirement, e.g. medicines, engineering, agriculture, paramedicines, computers etc. It thus becomes quite clear that to enter into any such vocational course an individual must have a knowledge of science and so the science education must be included in the school curriculum. In this age of science if we wish to prepare an individual for certain vocation it is essential that he be given a good education in science.

(*c*) Aesthetic Value

Knowledge of science develops in man a passion for truth and thus he has a passion for beauty. The English poet Keats has said, "Truth is Beauty". Science is basically unfolding of the mysteries of nature and nature is a store house of all the beautiful things. Thus we find that teaching of science of essential for developing an aesthetic sense in an individual. By enjoying the aesthetic aspects of his discoveries and inventions the scientist feel an intrinsic charm. The difference between a scientist and an artist is only superficial in that an artist aims more deliberately at beauty and a scientist attains and enjoys beauty through reasoning and truth.

(*d*) Practical Value

Scientific principles and laws find a large number of applications in our every day life. For proper utility of such applications some knowledge of science is necessary. At present we depend on scientific discoveries to a very large extent. Even a cursory and casual look around ourselves shows a lot of applications of science. For example electricity, electronics, communication, transport etc. We find that telephone has revolutionised the commercial world and has a profound effect on the market in general and stock market in particular. It has enabled us to talk to our friends or relatives sitting in remote corners of the world or even when they are a passenger on a liner and are in mid-sea. Aeroplane has reduced the distance and has helped to being countries together. Aeroplanes has fulfilled the long cherished desire of man to fly like a bird.

The most important practical value of science is felt in the world of medicines and health. Science has discovered a large number of new medicines which are used to cure such diseases which were considered as incurable only a flew decades ago. It has also given us new methods for prevention of diseases and we have been able to stop epidemics taking away a large number of human lives some contiguous diseases have been completely eradicated and in this way science has reduced the miseries of humanity and lengthened the average life of ordinary persons.

Science has also helped us overcome the problem of passing our leisure time and to make best use of it. Science has provided us with a large number of devices such as television, radio, cinema etc. which are a source of entertainment to all of us. These are also a source of knowledge and are used for spread of mass education and making the community aware of dangers of various ills. These devices are also used for eradication of various social evils. Science has also provided a large number of hobbies which we can usefully pursue in our leisure time, e.g. photography etc. The knowledge of science has also been found to a person whose hobby is gardening. Such a person will enjoy his hobby and will be benefitted more if he knows some thing about plant breeding, soil physics, chemical fertilizers etc.

(*e*) Moral Value

We have already learnt that a knowledge of science develops in us truthfulness and reasoning. Though such qualities may not make you a successful businessman or a successful politician according to present standards yet these are the very qualities which are desirable in all human beings. These qualities make the life worth living though they have lost their value in todays materialistic world. However none so far has said that training in truthfulness is bad.

(*f*) Psychological Value

Teaching of science is essential for developing scientific attitudes and scientific temper. Science helps us to develop positive attitudes such as open mindedness, reasoning etc. the learning of science is based on the fundamental principles of psychology *i.e.* 'learning by doing', 'learning by observing concrete and living specimens'. Being an activity oriented subject science helps to satisfy basic human desire of knowing about wonders of nature and so it satisfies common instincts as creativeness, self assertion, curiosity etc.

(*g*) Cultural Values

A study of the past scientists and their discoveries gives us an insight into the mode of their living, their spirit of sacrifice and their adventures. All such studies from the part of our cultural heritage and the study of this cultural past has a romance of its own. A knowledge of science develops in us a capacity to critically examining facts and arriving at logical conclusions. It also develops in us imagination power that is essential for proper solutions of various problems we actually face in our life.

(*h*) Adjustment in Modern Life

Science develops in us a *scientific attitude*. It also develops in an individual a specific procedure for attacking any problem. Such a specific procedure is called *'scientific method'*. Such a method prepares an individual to face the problems of life boldly and to solve them successfully. A person having scientific attitude has an open mind, a desire for accurate knowledge and a confidence to solve a problem using his sense of reasoning. A person having scientific attitude lives a peaceful and successful life.

1.5 CONCEPTS OF SCIENCES

Science has long been taught in different branches such as physics, Chemistry, Botany, Zoology etc. in a compartmentalised way. Each subject was taught separately and in isolation without bringing any correlation or integration between them. However in the later half of this century a new concept of science, with a completely compounded curriculum of all major branches has been evolved and courses were developed in *integrated science* (general science)

Concept of General Science

The first major international conference on the teaching of *integrated science*, sponsored by Unesco, was held in 1968 in Droujba

(Bulgaria) in cooperation with the International Council of Scientific Unions (ICSU), Committee on the Teaching of Science (CTS).

Five main conclusions that emerged from it are:

(*i*) Teaching of integrated science contributes towards general education, emphasizes the fundamental unity of science and leads towards an understanding of the place of science in contemporary society.

(*ii*) It avoids unnecessary repetitions and permits the introduction of intermediate disciplines.

(*iii*) It is necessary to omit some details in such an integrated course of science and so the contents of the course be judiciously chosen and be carefully compiled by collaboration between different teachers and other specialists

(*iv*) The extent of integration and the balance between integration and coordination will depend on the age of the students, the type of educational institutions and local conditions. At early stages of secondary education, a totally integrated course in experimental sciences is desirable.

(*v*) Science is an important part of primary education, particularly in arousing scientific curiosity and developing scientific attitudes and skills.

Another major conference for development of education in integrated science was held in Nijmegen (Netherlands) in 1978 which was organised by the International Council of Associations for Science Education (ICASE) in collaboration with Unesco.

The next significant international conference on integrated science teaching took place in Banglore (India) in 1985. It was organised by ICSU — CTS and its major aim was to identify practical ways in which education in science and technology can contribute to national development. Eight areas selected for the conference were food and agriculture; energy resources; land, water and mineral resources; health; industry and technology; the environment; information transfer and technology and ethics and social responsibility.

The most recent international gathering concerned with integrated science took place in Canberra (Australia) in July 1988. It made a distinction between 'Integrated' science and 'multidisciplinary' science.

An integrated approach to scientific endeavour after characterizes the highest level of research, where the work involves the efforts of the two or more specialists or teams of specialists having different disciplinary backgrounds and training. The results resemble a chemical compound, where the individual constituents or elements can no longer be recognized or physically separated. In this respect integrated science, where collaboration, often in parallel, leads to physical mixture; here the ingredients can be seen and disengaged. The properties of a compound transcend those of its elemental parts, where as those of mixture never do.

Now this new subject has developed to impart a unitary knowledge of science as a whole. It has a broad scope and can be applied to a broad range of interests. It has its own body of subject matter which is chosen to meet the needs of the students.

With the spread of 'education for all' and the growing awareness of the role and importance of science in modern world; it is not surprising to find the teaching of science gaining prominence in schools. Thus the number of science courses available at the primary or elementary level has grown dramatically. Most of them use environment as an important source. Many of the integrated science courses developed for secondary schools reflect aspects of science and society, some of the courses incorporate technology but a majority still concentrate on two or more usually, all three of the traditional branches of science (*i.e.* biology, physics, chemistry). The impact of computer and information technology is quite evident in some courses of integrated science. But the extent of the use of computers and suitability of the software deserve closer study, especially in relation to the whole range of practical activities undertaken by students.

The main characteristics of an integrated science course as outlined above can be summarised as under:

(*i*) It is free of any traditional boundries of different branches of science.

(*ii*) It is useful as a general education for every individual.

(*iii*) It covers Every Day Science for Every Body.

(*iv*) It helps common man in understanding his environment and help him to face his daily problems with confidence and solve them successfully.

John Murray has defined the general science as under:

"It is a course of scientific study and investigation which has its roots in common experiences of children and does not exclude any one of the fundamental special science".

In a recent review based on a study conducted by Unesco on '*The place of science and technology in school curricula*'. The matrix proposed by Abrahum Blum in 1973 has been used for purpose of definition. Blum's matrix has two axes; *scope* and *intensity*. Thus for inclusion, courses must cover at least two scientific disciplines and provide evidence of a substantial amount interweaving.

The introduction of general science course in Indian schools was strongly recommended by Secondary Education Commission (1952-53). Introduction of such a course at school level was also favoured during All India Seminar on Science Teaching held at Taradevi (1956). Teaching of general science was introduced, in India, as a compulsory subject at primary, middle and secondary level. It was however discontinued in middle and high school because of the opposition by various quarters.

1.6 VIEWS OPPOSING GENERAL SCIENCE

After introduction of General Science Course at various levels a general feeling was that the course has failed to achieve the objectives for which it was introduced. The following observations make the point clear.

A comprehensive report on science teaching in India was submitted by the UNESCO planning mission under the leadership of Prof. S.G. Shepovalonko. The mission stayed in India from December 23, 1963 to March 10, 1964. It recommended the abolition of General Science at the middle level. The commission also recommended the introduction of Physics and Biology from class VI and of chemistry from class VII.

The view expressed by Kothari Commission (1964-66) are as under.

"The General Science approach to teaching of science ...., has not proved successful as it Tends to make science appear somewhat formless and without structure and runs counter to its methodology. A disciplinary approach to science learning would, it is felt, be more effective in providing the necessary scientific base to young people".

1.7 DISCIPLINARY APPROACH

Keeping in view the opposition faced by the general science teaching the National Council of Educational Research and Training (N.C.E.R.T) introduced disciplinary approach to teaching of science at middle school stage on an experimental basis. However even this experimental replacement of general science was not suitable and was being replaced by Integrated Science. As has already been discussed the Integrated Science and a significant internal conference to give attention to Integrated Science took place in Banglore (India) in 1985. The main aim of this conference was to identify practical ways in which education in science and technology can contribute to national development.

The most recent international gathering of science educators to be concerned with integrated science took place in Canberra (Australia) in July, 1988. Here a seminar, jointly sponsored by ICASE and Unesco reviewed the place of integrated science course in education systems worldwide.

1.8 INTEGRATED SCIENCE CURRICULUM

Integrated approach to scientific endeavour in different from *multi-disciplinary science*.

The Journal *Interdisciplinary Science Reviews* contain, in the editorial of Vol. I, No. 1, the following reference to interdisciplinary science.

Increasing orientation towards interdisciplinary topics with in the scientific community requires an understanding by specialists in one field of the needs, problems and terminology of another field. Here the examples of Robert Boyle (1627 – 1691) and Alexander von Humboldt (1769 – 1859) are worth mentioning. These two scientists excelled in more than a single field of science and modern scientists may well be able to learn from their experience.

In recent times interdisciplinary research found its most wide spread use in operations research or operational research as it is called in United Kingdom, where it was originated by A.P. Rowe in 1937. He and his colleagues started teaching the intricacies of radar and they succeeded to such a large extent that by 1945 operational research activities had become a truly interdisciplinary effort of scientists and industrialists. Operations research is defined as the application of scientific method to the management of organized systems in which human behaviour plays an important part.

Systems engineering also use an interdisciplinary approach and tends to concentrate on technological innovations with less emphasis on the human factor. Systems analysis includes humanity in all its aspects and differs little from operations research as both fields have developed and matured through their outstanding achievements in industrial, military and space activities. The essence common to all is Interdisciplinary thinking and a fusion of efforts.

This understanding of integration can be widened to embrace many more scientific and human activities in wide variety of fields, including education.

Abraham Blum in 1973 proposed a Matrix as a criterion for including or excluding particular courses. This matrix has two axes: *Scope* and *Intensity*.

The *scope* of a course is the range of disciplines; scientific or social which it includes.

The *Intensity* measures the extent to which the subjects have been blended together to give a deliberate synthesis of the material.

Four discernibly different approaches are named as 'concept', the 'topic', the 'process' and the 'environmental' approach. There appears a trend towards adopting the 'process' approach and also for more courses to be oriented towards the 'environment. The latter development no doubt reflects the growing concern with science and society issues.

In most of the integrated science courses the curriculum has been developed keeping the following objectives in view.

(*i*) It should help develop a scientific attitudes.

(*ii*) It should the able to explain the relevance of science to every day life.

(*iii*) It must be able to create a feeling of reliance in the use of principles and practices of science.

(*iv*) It places due emphasis on the experimental work in science.

(*v*) It emphasises the unity of methods of various disciplines of science.

Nature of Curriculum

Curriculum development frequently originates within the confines of the country for which the learning material is devised, but it often borrows from extraneous sources. The courses in Integrated science have been developed in such a way so as to integrate science with the environment of child and not as an artificial integration of disciplines.

In Integrated science courses devised so far three categories of *intensity* can be identified: *coordinated, combined* and *amalgamated.*

In *coordinated courses* it is possible to identify distinct sections of chemistry, biology and physics. In *combined* courses, separate sciences are the starting point and the course in so designed that the three sciences are blended together.

In *amalgamated courses*, the ideas associated with separate sciences are used as required to give unified whole or a high degree of integration.

It can be easily assumed that amalgamated courses will be the hardest to devise and coordinated courses the easiest.

The science curriculum has been taken up in section 2.7.

CHAPTER 2

Aims and Objectives of Teaching Science

2.1 CRITERION USED FOR SELECTING

Aims of Teaching Science

The following criterion is used to select the aims and objectives of teaching science.

(*i*) This knowledge should should help the pupil in his daily life.

(*ii*) It should be related to the materials with which the pupil is familiar and should not be based on obsolete devices and ideas.

(*iii*) It should make the pupil fit for society.

(*iv*) It must provide him some practical experiences which form a part of his learning process.

(*v*) It should train the student in methods of science.

(*vi*) It should develop scientific attitude and science – related values among students.

(*vii*) It should inculcate scientific temper.

2.2 OBJECTIVES OF TEACHING SCIENCE

Objectives are the specific and precise behavioural outcome of teaching a particular topic in science. The objectives of a topic in science help in realising some general aim of teaching science. The characteristics of a good objective are as under:

(*i*) It should be specific and precise.

(*ii*) It should be attainable.

Bloom's Taxonomy of Objectives

Bloom's taxonomy of objectives is a classification of instructional objectives in a hierarchy. According to it the specific objectives have been classified into the following three categories:

(*i*) Cognitive domain objectives.

(*ii*) Affective domain objectives

(*iii*) Psychomotor domain objectives.

The cognitive domain objectives include knowledge, understandings, applications, analysis, synthesis and evaluation.

The effective domain objectives include the appreciations, values, attitudes, interests and feelings.

The psychomotor domain objectives include skills.

A brief discussion of these objectives is given below:

1. Knowledge

To impart knowledge in the basic aim of education and so it naturally is the basic aim of teaching of any subject including science. By imparting knowledge of science to the student it is expected that he acquires the knowledge of:

(*i*) natural phenomenon.

(*ii*) scientific terminology.

(*iii*) scientific concepts and formulea.

(*iv*) modern inventions of science.

(*v*) importance of animal life and plant life to man.

(*vi*) manipulation of nature by man.

(*vii*) correlation and inter-dependence of various branches of science.

(*viii*) environment.

Knowledge objective is considered to have been achieved if the student is able to recall and recognise scientific terms, facts, symbols, concepts etc.

2. Understanding

This objective considered to have been achieved if the student is able to:

(*i*) interpret charts, graphs, data, concept etc., correctly.

(*ii*) illustrate scientific terms, concepts, facts, phenomenons etc.

(*iii*) explain scientific facts, concepts, principles etc.

(*iv*) discriminate between different facts, concepts etc. that are closely related to each other.

(*v*) identify relationships between various facts, concepts, phenomenon etc.

(*vi*) change tables, symbols, terms etc. from any given form to some other desired form.

(*vii*) find faults, if any, in statements concepts etc.

3. Applications

This objective seems to be the most neglected one in our educational system. The common observation that supports it is that a science graduate fails to insert even a fuse wire in the electric circuit of his house. This objective is considered to have been achieved to a great extent if the pupil can:

(*i*) analyse a given data.

(*ii*) explain giving reasons various scientific phenomenon.

(*iii*) formulate hypothesis from his observations.

(*iv*) confirm or reject a hypothesis.

(*v*) correctly infer the observed facts.

(*vi*) find cause and effect relationship.

(*vii*) give new illustrations.

(*viii*) predict new happenings.

(*ix*) find relationships that exist between various facts, concepts, phenomenon learnt by him.

4. Skills

This objective can be considered to have been achieved if a pupil learns (*i*) handling piece of apparatus, (*ii*) assembling pieces of apparatus for experiment (*iii*) drawing diagrams and illustrations, (*iv*) constructing things, and (*v*) carrying our repairs of apparatus and appliances.

Thus here we aim to develop three types of skill in the pupil. These are (*a*) Drawing skill (*b*) manipulative skill and (*c*) observational and recording skill.

The drawing skill is considered to have been achieved if pupil is able to draw labelled sketches and diagrams quickly.

The manipulative skill is considered to have been achieved if pupil is able to

(*i*) keep and handle the apparatus or specimen properly.

(*ii*) improvise models and experiments.

(*iii*) observe various precautions while handling apparatus and doing experiments.

The observational and recording skill is considered to have been achieved if the pupil can

(*i*) read correctly the instrument or apparatus

(*ii*) record observations faithfully

(*iii*) make calculations correctly and

(*iv*) draw inferences correctly.

5. Interests

To achieve this objective the pupil is provided with scientific hobbies and other leisure time activities. By providing such activities our aim is to inculcate, among pupils, a living and substaining interest in environment in which he lives.

This aim is considered to have been achieved if the pupil becomes curious and develops such an interest in science that he is always eager and is on look out to:

(*i*) take to some interesting scientific hobby.

(*ii*) visit places of scientific interest.

(*iii*) undertake some science projects.

(*iv*) meet and interact some reputed person of science.

(*v*) read scientific literature.

(*vi*) collect specimen, scientific photographs, scientific biographics etc.

(*vii*) participate in science fair, science exhibition, science club etc.

(*viii*) actively participate in scientific debates, declamation contests, quiz etc.

6. Attitudes

Development of scientific attitude is one of the major objectives of teaching science. The development of scientific attitude makes pupil open minded, helps him to make critical observations, develops in him intellectual honesty, curiosity, unbiased and impartial thinking etc.

This objective is considered to have been achieved if a pupil

(*i*) becomes free of superstitions and prejudices

(*ii*) depends for his judgement only on verified facts and not on opinion

(*iii*) is readily willing to reconsider his own judgement when some more facts are brought to his notice

(*iv*) has an objective approach and

(*v*) is honest in recording and collecting scientific data.

7. Abilities

By the teaching of science we expect to develop the following abilities in the pupil

(*i*) ability to use scientific method

(*ii*) ability to use problem solving method

(*iii*) ability to process information

(*iv*) ability to report things in a technical language

(*v*) ability to collect scientific data from suitable source and to interpret it correctly

(*vi*) ability to organise science fair, science exhibition, science club etc.

8. Appreciation

To achieve this objective the teaching of science has to be done in an evolutionary way. For this the curriculum should include such topics where it is possible to reveal stirring biographical anecdotes, some scientific stories having some incidents of adventure, charm and romance. It is possible to achieve this objective by teaching history of science including life stories of some scientists. This objectives can also be achieved by telling the impact of modern science on life.

This objective of teaching science may be considered to have been achieved if the pupil:

(*i*) appreciates the contribution of various scientists to human progress.

(*ii*) appreciates the history of scientific development.

(*iii*) realises the importance of science in modern civilisation.

(*iv*) takes pleasure in understanding the progress made by science.

9. Providing Vocational Career

In the modern world majority of Career Courses depend to a large extent on the basic knowledge of science. Some Vocational Courses can be taken up only by students of science, *e.g.* Engineering, medicines, Agriculture etc. For various courses offered by I.T.I's the knowledge of science is the basic requirement. Thus science opens a vast field of opportunities for taking up any vocational course and choose a career. Not only this the knowledge of science develops in a pupil the manipulative skills and he can easily improvise apparatus and experiments and can use his knowledge and skill to make many a common things like ink, soap, candle, chalk, cosmetics, boot polish, nail polish etc. All these provide the pupil with a profitable leisure time work.

2.3 VIEWS OF SOME COMMITTEES ABOUT OBJECTIVES OF TEACHING SCIENCE

These very objectives of teaching science have been emphasised by various commissions. A brief summary of Taradevi Report and Kothari Commission is given here.

Taradevi Report

The important seminar on an all India basis was held at Taradevi (H.P) in 1956. The following is the summary of aims and objectives of teaching science as recommended at this seminar.

The aims and objectives of teaching science at primary, middle and secondary level are as under:

(*i*) *Primary Level.* The main aims of teaching of science at primary level are:

(*i*) to arouse and maintain interest in nature and physical environment.

(*ii*) to arouse love for nature and the habit of conserving nature and natural resources.

(*iii*) to inculcate habit of observation, exploration, classification and a systematic way of thinking.

(*iv*) to develop manipulative powers and creative and inventive faculties.

(*v*) to inculcate habits of healthful living.

(*ii*) *Middle School Level.* At middle school level, teaching of science aims at the following in addition to the aims given above:

(*i*) it aims at acquisition of a lot of information about nature and science.

(*ii*) it aims at developing ability of make generalisations and use them for solving problems in every day life.

(*iii*) it aims at understanding the impact of science on our way of life.

(*iv*) it aims to develop an interest in various scientific hobbies and

(*v*) inspire pupils by telling them stories of some great scientists and their discoveries.

(*iii*) *High and Higher Secondary Level.* At this stage the aims of teaching science are:

(*i*) to familiarise the student with his surroundings and to make him understand the impact of science on society and thus enable him to adjust himself with his environment.

(*ii*) to familiarise him with 'scientific method' and thus to help him to develop the scientific attitude

(*iii*) to make him understand the evolution of science in the historical perspective.

Kothari Commission (1964-66)

An education commission was constituted under the chairmanship of Dr. D.S. Kothari and it made the following recommendations in its report.

(*i*) The teaching science in primary schools should aim at developing proper understanding of main facts, concepts, principles and processes in physical and biological environments.

(*ii*) The science education be imparted making use of both deductive and inductive approaches, however more emphasis be given to deductive approach.

Following recommendations were made by Kothari Commission (1964-1966) for different school stages:

1. *Lower Primary Stage*

(*i*) At this stage emphasis be put on the child's environment – social, physical and biological.

(*ii*) In classes (I) and (II) more attention be paid to cleanliness, formation of healthy habits and development of power of observation.

(*iii*) In classes (III) and (IV) more emphasis be given on personal hygiene and sanitation.

(*iv*) In class (IV) Roman alphabets be taught to the students as these are the internationally accepted symbols for units of scientific measurements. Moreover the symbols of elements and compounds are also make use of Roman alphabets.

(*v*) At this stage an effort be made to develop proper understanding of important facts, concepts, principles etc. that we come across in physical and biological sciences.

2. *Higher Primary Stage:* The teaching of science at this stage should emphasize on the acquisition of knowledge alongwith the ability of logical thinking and drawing conclusions for taking decisions at a higher level. At this stage a disciplinary approach of teaching science is favoured instead of an integrated science teaching. The teaching of physics, chemistry, botany, etc. is likely to develop more effective scientific base.

3. *Secondary Stage*

(*i*) At this stage science be taught as a discipline of mind and a preparation of higher education.

(*ii*) In lower secondary classes (class IX and X) the subjects of physics, chemistry, biology and earth sciences be made compulsory.

(*iii*) At higher secondary stage diversification of courses and provision for specialisation be allowed.

Recommendations of N.C.E.R.T.

The objectives of teaching science according to various recommendations of N.C.E.R.T. may be summarised as under:

(*i*) To explore immediate environment of the pupil.

(*ii*) To observe, record, report accurately in oral, written and graphic form.

(*iii*) To formulate precise questions about various things in environment.

(*iv*) To collect information from various sources and use it in a given situation.

(*v*) To classify objects, events, phenomenon.

(*vi*) To arrange objects and data in a sequence so as to assertain a pattern.

(*vii*) To analyse data and make inference.

(*viii*) To find some cause–effect relationship from the data available.

(*ix*) To make predictions.

(*x*) To design simple experiments.

(*xi*) To solve problems.

(*xii*) To develop an objective attitude towards experimental evidences and to make decisions on the basis of facts and data.

(*xiii*) To understand the role of Indian scientists in the development of science.

(*xiv*) To make a judicious use of national resources after their proper identification.

(*xv*) To be careful to avoid any wastage of natural resources and to take necessary steps for prevention of pollution.

(*xvi*) To correlate the knowledge of science and technology to economic and social development of the community.

(*xvii*) To place due emphasis on scientific knowledge in everyday life.

(*xviii*) To make proper use of scientific knowledge for development of desired social and moral values.

(*xix*) To develop instrumental, communicational and problem solving skills.

(*xx*) To develop scientific attitude, spirit of cooperation, scientific temper and scientific approach.

2.4 SCIENTIFIC ATTITUDE

One of the major aims of teaching science is the development of *scientific attitude* in the pupil. Following are some of the various aspects included in the scientific attitude:

(*i*) Making pupils open minded.

(*ii*) Helping pupils make critical observations.

(*iii*) Developing intellectual honesty among pupils.

(*iv*) Developing curiosity among pupils.

(*v*) Developing unbiased and impartial thinking.

(*vi*) Developing reflective thinking.

NSSE (National Society of the Study of Education) has defined scientific attitudes as "open mindedness, a desire for accurate knowledge, confidence in procedures for seeking knowledge and the expectation that the solution of the problem will come through the use of verified knowledge".

The views regarding scientific attitude expressed at a work shop conducted by the National Council of Educational Research and Training (NCERT) at Chandigarh in 1971 can be summarised as follows. A pupil who has developed scientific attitude.

(*i*) is clear and precise in his activities and makes clear and precise statements.

(*ii*) always bases his judgement on verified facts and not on opinions.

(*iii*) prefers to suspend his judgement if sufficient data is not available.

(*iv*) is objective in his approach and behaviour.

(*v*) is free from superstitions.

(*vi*) is honest and truthful in recording and collecting scientific data.

(*vii*) after finishing his work takes care to arrange the apparatus, equipments etc. at their proper places.

(*viii*) shows a favourable reaction towards efforts of using science for human welfare.

2.5 TECHNIQUES FOR DEVELOPING SCIENTIFIC ATTITUDES

In the previous pages an effort was made to define the term '*scientific attitude*'. By developing scientific attitude in a person certain mind-sets are created in a particular direction. Such mind-sets may be developed either by direct teaching in schools or by out of school experiences gained by the pupil. Though out of school experiences contribute to a large extent yet according to *Curtis* direct teaching does modify the attitude of young pupil.

Tyler also made some suggestions for planning learning experiences in order to inculcate scientific attitude in the pupil. These are summarised below:

(*i*) The increase in the degree of consistency of the environment helps in developing and inculcating scientific attitude in the pupil.

(*ii*) The scientific attitude can be inculcated in a pupil by providing him more opportunities for making satisfying adjustments to attitude situations.

(*iii*) The scientific attitude can also be developed in the pupil by providing him opportunity for the analysis of problem or situation so that a pupil may understand and then rest intellectually in desirable attitude.

Role of Science Teacher

The major role can be played by the science teacher in developing scientific attitudes among his students and this he can do by manipulating various situations that infuse among the pupils certain characteristics of scientific attitudes. He can also help in developing a scientific attitude among his students if he possesses and practices various elements of these attitudes. The practical examples given by the teacher leaves an indelible mark on the personality of his students.

Teacher can use one or more of the ways for developing scientific attitude among his pupils.

(*i*) *Making use of Planned Exercises*: A large number of exercises for development of certain scientific attitudes are reported by various journals and magazines. Teacher can frequently use such exercises for developing certain scientific attitudes among the pupils. He can also make use of cuttings from newspapers and science magazines and can display such materials on bulletin board so that it is used again and again for direct teaching.

Exercises which are always included in good text books can also be used by the teacher for developing scientific attitude among his pupils.

(*ii*) *Wide Reading*: On the basis of a study conducted by him, *Curtis* reported, that those pupil who engage themselves in wide reading in science, develop scientific attitudes more than those who study only one textbook. Thus a teacher should encourage his students to read library books and supplementary books on science. For this it is essential that each school at least has a science corner in its library. The teacher himself must be in habit of making proper use of science library so that his students get encouragement for use of science library. The teacher himself be familiar with the latest new titles in his subject and he willing to share his joys of new readings with his pupils. He should refer some suitable books to his students.

Writing about teachers, Dr. Rabinder Nath Tagore has observed, "A teacher can never truly teach unless he is still learning himself. A lamp can never light another unless it continues to burn its own flame. The teacher who has come to the end of his subject, who has no living traffic with his knowledge, but merely repeats his lessons to his students, can only load their minds. He cannot quicken them".

(*iii*) *Proper use of Practicals Period:* A student of science gets many an opportunities for learning scientific attitudes during his practical periods. It is for the teacher to properly use such opportunities for developing scientific attitudes amongst his pupils. Teacher should take extra care to state the problem of the experiment and should present hypotheses on solution. He should practice the proper method of testing the hypothesis. He should actively participate in discussion and interpretation of results after the experiment. He must inculcate in his students the habit to postpone judgements in the absence of sufficient evidence to support a hypothesis.

(*iv*) *Personal Example of the Teacher*: Personal example of the teacher is perhaps the single greatest force that is helpful in inculcating the scientific attitudes amongst his pupils. Psychologists have found a great tendency amongst the students to copy their teachers. In this regard some have stated, "As is the teacher, so is the student". It is therefore essential that science teacher is free from bias and prejudices while dealing with his pupils. He should have an open mind and be critical in thought and action in his everyday dealings. He should be totally free from superstitions and unfounded beliefs and should be objective and impartial in his approach to his everyday problems. He should be truthful and should have faith in cause and effect relationship.

(*v*) *Study of Superstitions:* There are different types of superstitions that still prevail in Indian society. Simply talking of these superstitions and calling them bad and out of date, will not leave a lasting impression on the minds of the pupils. It will be more useful if the teacher can encourage at least a few of his students to carry out practicals on some popular superstitions such as that the presence of a broken mirror in any home leads to disharmony in that home or that if a cat crosses your way when you are going out for some work, then your work will not be done on that day etc. etc.

Such beliefs can easily be discarded by a student if he keeps a broken mirror at his home and finds to his satisfaction that it has not created any type of disharmony in his home. Similarly other superstitions and misbeliefs can be tested and easily discarded by a student of science. Various researches carried out in the field have drawn the same conclusion *i.e.* by practical survey and study of such common beliefs, students have developed permanent mind-sets or attitudes towards such superstitions.

(*vi*) *Co-curriculum Activities in Science*: Various co-curricular activities such as organising science club, hobbies club, science society, photographic club, organising scientific tours and excursions etc. can be taken up by science teacher. Such activities should be properly organised by science teacher under his direct supervision but students be given enough freedom to plan their activities. It will help inculcate in students some desirable scientific attitudes. Co-curricular activities may include making of scientific charts and models, making of improvised science apparatus etc.

(*vii*) *Atmosphere of the Class:* A proper atmosphere in the class room provided a desirable atmosphere for inculcating of certain scientific attitudes in the pupils. By a proper class atmosphere we mean that the room is properly arranged and suitably decorated in such a manner that it provides an incentive to the pupil to inculcate the habit of cleanliness and orderliness. In addition to such a congenial physical atmosphere of the class room, the teacher's behaviour also contributes to the development of proper class room atmosphere. For inculcating the scientific attitudes amongst his pupils teacher should encourage them in their various activities. He should also take care to see that his lessons contain are such as to encourage the students to ask a large number of intelligent questions. He should feel pleasure in answering and explaining such questions and must not snub his pupils for asking so many questions.

2.6 SCIENTIFIC METHOD

It has already been pointed out that two basic aims of teaching science and (*i*) development of scientific attitude and (*ii*) training in scientific methods.

In previous section we have discussed same ways for developing scientific attitude and in this section our aim is to concentrate mainly on training in scientific methods.

A 'scientific method' is 'a method which is used for solving a problem scientifically'. It is also referred to as 'the method of science' or 'the method of a scientist. Sometimes it is called as 'problem solving method'. So far it has not been possible to arrive at any commonly agreed definition of scientific method.

The scientific method of teaching science is based upon the process of finding out results by attacking a problem in definite steps, therefore there cannot be any one 'particular method' but such methods have certain common characteristics.

According to Fitzpatrick, "Science is a cumulative and endless series of emperical observations which result in the formation of concepts and theories, with both concepts and theories being subject to modification in the light of further empirical observation. Science is both the study of knowledge and the process of acquiring and refining knowledge". From this it becaúse quite clear that student of science be exposed to the scientific method of finding out. Scientific method helps to develop in a student the power of reasoning, critical thinking and application of scientific knowledge. It also helps in developing positive attitudes amongst the pupils. A list of such traits as given by Woodburn and Oburn is as under:

(*i*) A scientist must have an unsatiable curiosity, inquisitiveness and a spirit of adventure.

(*ii*) He should be capable of independent thinking and be ready to abandon the disproved.

(*iii*) He should be knowledgeable, enlightened and informed.

(*iv*) He should possess a power of sound judgement and prudent foresight.

(*v*) He should possess a high degree of perseverance.

Steps of Scientific Method

Since we don't have any single well defined scientific method so we cannot have any well defined fixed steps for a scientific method. However in general the scientific method of teaching science proceeds in the following steps:

(*i*) Problem in an area of science learning is identified and well stated.

(*ii*) Relevant data is collected.

(*iii*) Certain hypothesis are proposed for testing.

(*iv*) Experiments are set and done to test the proposed hypothesis.

(*v*) Prediction of other observable phenomenon are deduced from the hypothesis.

(*vi*) Occurence or non-occurence of predicted phenomenon is observed.

(*vii*) From observations, the conclusions are drawn to accept, reject or modify the proposed hypothesis.

Thus the scientific method is a sequenced and structured way of finding out the results through experiments. Various steps of scientific method are discussed here.

(*i*) *Statement of the Problem*: A student comes across so many things which arouse his curiosity and he has a large number of questions to ask. A good science teacher always encourages his students to ask questions and tries to answer them in a simple and understandable manner. However in answering a particular question the teacher brings to fore many new problems and it has rightly been said that, "when we double the known, we quadruple the unknown".

Most of the question asked are about 'what?', 'why?' or 'how?' type and these can be conveniently classified as under.

(*i*) 'what' type of questions are *predictive*

(*ii*) 'why' type of questions are *explanatory*

(*iii*) 'how' type of questions are *inventory*

The most important thing in a scientific method is a simple and well defined statement of the problem. The statement of the problem be such that it clearly defines the scope of the problem as also its limitations.

(*ii*) *Data Collection:* When the problem has been stated in clear terms an effort be made to collect the data from as many different source as is possible. Such data may be available in books in science, library which are an important source for data collection. Data may be collected by use of certain instruments etc. and observations. In data collection an effort be made to minimise the errors that are likely to be caused due to apparatus and instruments used *(mechanical errors)* and those which are likely to be caused due to personal bias *(personal errors)*.

(*iii*) *Proposing a Hypotheses:* On the basis of collected data a tentative hypothesis is proposed for testing. A hypothesis is in fact a certain tentative solution to the problem. The hypothesis should be proposed only after an objective analysis of the available data because any number of hypothesis can be proposed for a problem. For an objective analysis the student be given a training so that he is free from all his bias towards the problem.

(*iv*) *Conducting Experiments:* After a hypothesis has been proposed suitable experiments are designed to test the validity of the hypothesis. From the observations of such experiments the validity of the hypothesis is tested. The experiments will show the occurence or non-occurence of the expected phenomenon and from this we will be able to accept or reject or modify the hypothesis.

Advantages of Scientific Method

Some of the advantages of scientific method are:

(*i*) Students learn science by their own experiences and the teacher is just a guide who provides them an opportunity and proper environment for learning science.

(*ii*) It trains the students to identify and formulate scientific problems.

(*iii*) It gives enough training to students in techniques of information processing.

(*iv*) It develops in students the power of logical thinking as he is required to interpret data in a logical way.

(*v*) It helps to develop an intellectual honesty in the student because he is required to accept or reject the hypothesis on the basis of evidences available.

(*vi*) It helps the students to learn to see relationships and patterns amongst things and variables.

(*vii*) It provides the students a training in the methods and skills of discovering new knowledge.

Disadvantages of Scientific Method

Some important disadvantages of scientific methods are as under:

(*i*) It is a long drawn out and time consuming process.

(*ii*) It can never be a full fledged method of learning science.

(*iii*) Majority of science teachers cannot implement it successfully because of their back of exposure to such a method.

(*iv*) It is not suitable for all students as it suits only bright and creative students.

2.7 SCIENCE CURRICULUM

Curriculum is a gist of lessons and topics which are expected to the covered in a specified period of time in any class. However this traditional concept of curriculum has undergone a change in modern times. Now curriculum refers to the totality of experiences that a child receives through various class room activities as also from activities in library, laboratory, workshop, assembly hall, play fields etc. Thus according to modern concept curriculum includes the whole life of the school. Thus those activities which were previously referred to as co-curricular or extra-curricular activities have now become curricular activities.

According to this concept the science curriculum can be considered to include the subject matter in science, various co-curricular activities in science etc.

Curriculum is derived from Latin word "currere" meaning "to run". Thus curriculum in the medium to realise the goals and objectives of teaching a particular course of study.

Science Curriculum

Before venturing to form a curriculum in science for being taught in our schools we have to take into consideration the kind of school population and other requirements. We shall also have to keep in mind the aim of teaching science in our schools. It is our endeavour to include in the science curriculum various natural phenomenon, physical laws and some simple applications of science that we come across in our every day life. More over since knowledge of science in the basis of various vocational courses (*e.g.* medicines and engineering etc.) so the curriculum in science must also such topics as are required for success in such a vocational course.

For formation of curriculum in science we can easily classify the school population in two classes as under:

(*i*) Those students who complete their education at the primary or middle stage, and

(*ii*) Those who continue in high/higher secondary schools.

Only a small fraction of the students who continue their education in high/higher secondary school offer for science courses.

The curriculum in science should be different for the above two classes of school population. For those students who are not likely to continue with education after middle stage we should offer a general science course that may be of use to them as a part of sound liberal education. For those students who are likely to continue with science subjects at high/higher secondary stage we should offer a course that provides specialised knowledge of one or more branches of science.

If we look at the existing science curriculum we find it to be defective as it is a hotch-potch mixture of various branches of science.

It appears that it has no definite goals to achieve and so it defeats the very purpose of teaching science. It burdens the students mind with dead information and does not provide him any encouragement for taking up creative and useful activities.

The Secondary Education Commission (1953) refers to the criticism of the existing curriculum as under:

(*i*) It is a narrowly conceived curriculum.

(*ii*) It is theoretical and bookish.

(*iii*) It is over crowded.

(*iv*) It does not provide rich and significant subject matter.

(*v*) In it there is inadequate provision for practical work.

(*vi*) It fails to develop a balanced personality.

(*vii*) It fails to cater to the various needs and capacities of adolescents.

(*viii*) It is an examination dominated curriculum.

The Kothari Commission (1966) also considered it and according to it the dissatisfaction with science curriculum in our schools may be due to the following two factors.

(*i*) The tremendous explosion in knowledge, in various branches of science, that has occurred in recent years. This explosion in knowledge has led to reformulation of some of the basic concepts in physical sciences, biological sciences and social sciences. This advancement in knowledge of science has intended the already existing gulf between the school and the university in major academic disciplines.

(*ii*) There is a rethinking in the duration of education that is imparted in ordinary schools. There is a unanimity in the views of educationist all of whom now favour the increase in the period of general education thereby postponing the entry into specialised courses of study. This has necessitated the introduction of some more significant topics in an already over packed school curriculum. For this we have to discard some topics from the existing curriculum.

2.8 PRINCIPLES OF CURRICULUM FORMATION

There are certain basic principles of curriculum planning which should form the basis for the formation of a good science curriculum. These are:

1. *The principle of child centredness*: The curriculum should be based on the present needs and circumstances of the child.
2. *Curriculum should provide a fulness of experience for children.*
3. *The curriculum should be dynamic and not static.*
4. *It should be related to every day life.*
5. *It must take into account the economic aspect of life of the people to whom an educational institution belongs.*
6. *The curriculum should be realistic and rationalistic.*
7. *While forming the curriculum a balance be struck between the education of nature and education of man.*
8. *It should lay emphasis on learning to live rather than on living to learn.*
9. *In curriculum such activities must be included, which help in preserving and transmitting the traditions knowledge and standards of conduct on which our civilisation depends.*
10. *It should be elastic and flexible.*
11. *It should be well integrated.*
12. *It should provide both for uniformity and variety.*
13. *It should be able to serve the needs of community.*

As far as science curriculum is concerned it should be elastic and variable, child-centred, community centred, activity centred. It should be such as to be use for adjustment in life and helps to integrate the activities of the child with his environment. It should be helpful to conserve and transmit the traditions, culture and civilisation. It must help in arousing the creative faculties of the children.

2.9 APPROACHES TO CURRICULUM PLANNING

There are a number of approaches to curriculum planning in science. The extremes of such approaches are given on page 36 (Table 2.1).

Actually no single way of curriculum planning exclusively based on one approach can fulfil the curricular needs of pupils. It is always better to combine different approaches to plan an effective curriculum in science.

TABLE 2.1

The Extreme of Curriculum Formation

One extreme	*Other extreme*
Integrated	Disciplinary
Child-centred	Teacher-centred
Flexible	Structured
Process-based	Content-based
Conceptual	Factual

2.10 CURRICULUM STYLES

Curriculum can be classified as:

(*i*) Instrumental curriculum.

(*ii*) Interactive curriculum.

(*iii*) Individualistic curriculum.

Instrumental Curriculum

In this type of curriculum more emphasis is placed on the utility value or vocational value of science. It makes learning an intense competition among students.

The basic approach in such a curriculum is disciplinary and emphasises the acquisition of knowledge or information. The role of teacher is that of a dominant teacher in such a curriculum.

Interactive Curriculum

This type of curriculum is society oriented and lays more emphasis on the social development of child. In this type of curriculum class room instructions becomes an interactive or a cooperative process. The approach is interdisciplinary and the curriculum is loosely structured and consists of learning packages.

Individualistic Curriculum

In this type of curriculum more emphasis is placed on the personal development of the individual and it is based on inter-disciplinary approach. It helps to develop creativity in the individual. This type of curriculum is based on self-calculation by the student.

2.11 CURRICULUM IN GENERAL SCIENCE CONTENT

Keeping in view that the major aim of teaching science is to acquaint the students with himself and his environment (*i.e.* things around him), it is desirable if the student is imparted a working knowledge of almost all the main branches of science. To achieve this the general science course should include topics from the following branches of science:

(*i*) Physics (*ii*) Chemistry (*iii*) Botany (*iv*) Zoology (*v*) Geography (*vi*) Physiology (*vii*) Astronomy (*viii*) Geology and (*ix*) Home Science (for girls).

For selecting different topics, from various branches of science, for inclusion in general science curriculum the following points be given due consideration.

(*i*) Content should be selected in terms of broad concepts and principles of science.

(*ii*) Content should be related to the different age-groups and daily life.

(*iii*) It should be able to serve the needs of the community.

(*iv*) It should be very closely associated with the environment.

(*v*) It should be such as could be dealt within the available time under existing conditions of staff, equipment etc.

Arrangement of Material

In case of general science curriculum the best arrangement is the one based on 'topics' or 'units' because such an arrangement provides a natural method of learning. In such an arrangement the 'units' should be such as are of immediate interest to the student and are related to the local environment and community. 'Topics' should arise out of environment and experiences of the pupil and the study material should be arranged around these topics in such a fashion that it brings about a closer integration between various branches of science. It should also bring about a greater correlation with life situations and every day experiences of the child.

The general science course for elementary schools can be organised around the following main units:

(*i*) Living things, (*ii*) Earth and universe, and (*iii*) Matter and Energy.

Alternatively it can be organised around the following main units:

(*i*) Our surroundings.
(*ii*) Nature of things.
(*iii*) Energy and work.
(*iv*) Life.
(*v*) Human machine.

The curriculum must include some experiments for the children in addition to subject matter. It should also indicate various related activities for different topics. Following example illustrates it.

Content	*Demonstration*	*Experiment*	*Activities*
Unit *Our surroundings*			
(*i*) The earth, rocks and soil, different kinds of rocks and minerals	(*i*) Three classes of rocks (*ii*) Identification of minerals (*iii*) Making artificial rocks	(*i*) Study of some rocks (*ii*) Making a model of volcano	Visit to hilly and arid areas and collecting rocks and minerals

All India Seminar on Science Teaching has suggested the following for bringing about a closer cooperation between various branches of science. The units be

(*i*) Environment centred
(*ii*) Life centred
(*iii*) Environment and life centred

Units based on Environment-centred Topics

Unit I The atmosphere
Unit II Water, Elixir of life
Unit III The earth

Unit IV	Heat
Unit V	Light
Unit VI	Metals and Non-metals
Unit VII	Work and energy
Unit VIII	Means of transport and communication
Unit IX	Plant and animal life
Unit X	The study of the Body Machine.

Units based on Life-centred Topics

Unit I	Importance of science in our life
Unit II	The air
Unit III	The water
Unit IV	The food
Unit V	The clothes
Unit VI	The homes
Unit VII	The machines
Unit VIII	Power and Energy
Unit IX	Protection from disease
Unit X	Biological resources
Unit XI	Mineral resources
Unit XII	Means of transport
Unit XIII	Means of communication
Unit XIV	Our universe
Unit XV	Story of life.

Units based on Environment and Life Centred Topics

Unit I	Importance of science
Unit II	Human body, the machine and its working
Unit III	Our health
Unit IV	Our biological resources and their use for better living
Unit V	Our mineral resources and their use for better living
Unit VI	Energy and machines
Unit VII	Time, measurement and mass production
Unit VIII	The weather
Unit IX	The solar system, stars and other universes

Unit X Science in daily life

(*a*) Heating our homes

(*b*) Lighting our homes

(*c*) Electronics in our homes

(*d*) Sound in homes.

2.12 CURRICULUM IN SCIENCE FOR DIFFERENT STAGES

1. Primary Stage

The students at primary stage are in the age group 5-10 and so they are quite immature thus they be given only a formal education in science. At this stage it is desirable to develop the subject matter under the following heads:

(*i*) Living things

(*ii*) Universe

(*iii*) Matter and Energy.

The curriculum must provide for some students activity in addition to the subject matter. Of the estimated 100 hours allotted to teaching of science in a class about 20 hours be spent on excusions and visits, about 50 hours on projects and other activities and the remaining 30 hours be given to class room teaching.

Kothari Commission (1966) recommended as under:

(*i*) In lower primary classes, the focus should be on the child's environment – social, physical and biological

(*ii*) In classes I and II accent should be on (*a*) cleanliness (*b*) Formation of healthy habits (*c*) development of lower of observation.

(*iii*) In addition to emphasising the above qualities in class III and IV the information be provided about (*a*) Personal hygiene (*b*) Sanitation (*c*) Plants and animals in surroundings of the child (*d*) Air (*e*) Water (*f*) Weather (*g*) Earth (*h*) Simple Machines (*i*) Care of body (*j*) Heavenly Bodies.

(*iv*) To provide direct and valuable experiences of natural phenomenon it is recommended that school gardening be encouraged.

2. Middle Stage

At this stage it is desirable to place more emphasis to the acquisition of knowledge and the ability to think logically. It should also be the aim at this stage that a student in encouraged to draw conclusion and take decisions. It would be desirable if science at this stage is taught as physics, chemistry and biology etc. At this stage this disciplinary approach will be more effective.

Keeping in view the above recommendations of Kothari Commission (1966) science is taught as physics, chemistry and Biology in our schools.

However now NCERT has framed a syllabus for integrated science course from class VI, VII and VIII and the outlines of this newly framed curriculum are given below:

Integrated Science Curriculum

Objectives:

1. To put emphasise on the relevance of science to daily life.
2. To develop scientific attitudes.
3. To create an environment that is conducive to more reliance on the use of principles and practices of science.
4. To familiarise the students with different natural phenomena.
5. To emphasise the experimental nature of science.
6. To emphasise the unity of methods of various disciplines of science.

Nature of the Course. In this we have tried to integrate science with the environment of the child rather than making an artificial integration of various disciplines of science. The students with the back ground of general science at primary level, would find this course as a continuation of their earlier knowledge. They will also be mentally prepared to offer science courses at secondary level. NCERT have developed Composite Integrated Science Kit alongwith text-books for classes VI, VII and VIII.

3. High School Stage

The recommendations of Kothari Commission (1966) are as under:

(*i*) In classes IX and X it would be desirable to introduce newer concepts of Physics, Chemistry and Biology. Moreover the experimental approach to learning of science be emphasised at this stage.

(*ii*) It was also recommended that provisions be made for advanced courses in science subjects for talented students in some selected secondary schools. Such schools be provided with necessary facilities of staff and laboratories.

(*iii*) As far as possible science teaching in rural areas be linked to agriculture and in urban areas to technology.

The content of specialized science courses in physics, chemistry and biology should be such as to useful for further vocational studies in the respective fields. An effort be made to present the subject matter as a synthetic whole and not merely as collection of few principles and facts. Various examples and illustrations be given from daily life of students and from their local environment. For this purpose the subject matter be arranged around broad based units.

National Policy on Education as given by Government of India states as under.

"With a view to the growth of the national economy, science education and research should receive high priority. Science and mathematics should form an integral part of general education till the end of school stage".

With the above policy statements in view new Integrated Science Curriculum were prepared by NCERT. Outlines of these are given below:

2.13 NEW INTEGRATED SCIENCE CURRICULUM OF NCERT

Class VI

1. Measurement
2. Materials around us
3. Separation of substances

4. Changes around us
5. Motion, force and pressure
6. Simple machines
7. The universe
8. The living world
9. Study of structures and functions in plants and animals
10. Food and health
11. Man's dependence on plants and animals and the balance of nature
12. Environment
13. Water
14. Energy.

Class VII

1. Motion, mass and friction
2. Pressure and buoyancy
3. Heat
4. Light
5. Sound
6. Current Electricity
7. Static Electricity
8. Magnetism
9. Nature and composition of substances
10. Air
11. Water
12. Acids, bases and salts
13. Preservation of self
14. Population Explosion
15. Pollution.

Class VIII

1. Light
2. Electricity
3. Electrical energy
4. Electrical magnetism

5. Structure of atom
6. Nuclear energy
7. Carbon
8. Our living world
9. Cell and tissue
10. Reproduction
11. Growth and development
12. Heredity and variation
13. Organic evolution
14. Materials
15. Agricultural practices and implements
16. Our crops
17. Improvement of crop production
18. Some useful plants and animals
19. Animal husbandry
20. Conservation of natural resources
21. Science in human welfare.

2.14 PLACE OF SCIENCE IN SOME COUNTRIES

Before we close this chapter let us look at the place of science in school in some countries.

Africa

Science in Primary classes: In most of the African countries the Science allotted to teaching of sciences is between 1.4 and 1.8 hours. In Nigeria 4.3 hours per week are devoted to primary school science, in Liberia 4 hours, in Uganda 3.8 hours, in Lesotho only 1 hour per week is given. Practical work is not time tabled in primary schools in Africa as in other countries. Pupil activity and demonstrations by the teacher are encouraged and are facilitated in countries such as Lesotho.

Science in Secondary Classes: Most of the countries require pupil to take a 2-, 3- or 4-year course in integrated science on entry into secondary schools. In place of integrated science course in some countries general science course is allowed. However in Mali pupils in grade 7, 8, 9 are required to take three subjects biology, chemistry and physical science. In Niger, biology only is required in grade 7 and 8.

In last 2 or 3 years of secondary school the usual practice is to provide separate courses in physics, chemistry and biology.

The need for practical work is science is almost universally recognised at the secondary stage. In Botswana all science lessions are given in a laboratory and in double periods so as to permit practical work as the need arises. In Liberia, 1 hour per week is allotted to each physics, chemistry and biology for practicals in grades 10, 11 and 12. In Mauritius, the time allotted to practical work rises grade by grade. One period per week in grade 10, two in grade 11 and upto four in grades 12 and 13.

Arab States

Science in Primary Classes: Except Jordan all countries teach science from grade 1 to 6. Most of the countries offer integrated science course for 1.5 to 2 hours rising to about 2.5 hours in grades 3 to 6.

Science in Secondary Classes: Most of the countries provide a course of integrated science in grades 7, 8 and 9 and offer separate sciences in grades 10, 11 and 12. Three hours per week is allowed to cover integrated course and 2 hours per week to each of the separate science courses.

In Jordan integrated course is retained in grade 10 and separate courses are offered only in grade 11, 12. Morocco and Tunisia offer a combination of physical sciences and biological sciences courses from grade 8 to 12. Practical work is given due importance and is time tabled in grades 10, 11, 12 and absorbs about half of the allotted time to science.

Asia and the Pacific

Science in Primary Classes: Science is taught from class 1 to 10 in almost all the countries and it is a common practice to devote 1 hour per week to science topics. The courses are generally in *integrated science* which is doubtless based on or closely related to the experiences of the young child.

Science in Secondary Classes: In early secondary stage most of the countries favour an integrated science course. Integrated science teaching is followed from grade 6 or 7 to 10 in Afghanistan, Australia, Malaysia, Nepal, New Zealand, Pakistàn and Sri Lanka. In Indonesia and Korea integrated science courses are offered in grades 7, 8 and 9. Singapore has a 2 year course taken in grades 7 and 8.

In Japan, in grades 7 to 10, two science courses are followed. One in physical sciences and one in which combines biology and geology.

In India a two-subject approach is found in grades 9 and 10 involving physical sciences and biology.

In China separate sciences are preferred throughout. In grade 7, biology in studied; in grade 8, biology and physics; in grade 9, physics, chemistry and physical sciences; in grade 10, physics and chemistry; in grade 11, chemistry and physics and in grade 12, physics and biology.

The three traditional subjects physics, chemistry and biology are offered as optional subjects during the late secondary school years in almost all the countries of the region. Some countries provide an even wider choice. For example in Australia in addition to separate sciences, courses are offered in integrated sciences such as physical sciences, geology and environmental sciences. In Afghanistan astronomy is offered in grade 10.

In secondary school, practical work is quite prominent. In some countries, the deliberate allocation of time to permit students to conduct their own experiments is surprisingly high. In Australia one half of the total time allotted to science courses is absorbed by practical work.

In India, two periods per week are given to practical work in grades 9 and 10, four periods per week in grades 11 and 12. In Pakistan 2 hours and 40 minutes are allotted to each of physics, chemistry and biology in grades 11 and 12.

In Philippines, where chemistry is taught in third secondary year and physics in fourth, seven periods per week are allotted, two for lectures and five for experimental work.

In Sri Lanka, 3 hours per week are spent on practical work in each science subject in grades 11 and 12.

Europe

Primary Classes: In a number of countries science topics form part of 'environment studies' during early primary school years. In later years science in taught as integrated science course.

Secondary Classes: In most of the countries various combinations of science subjects are offered but generally options are allowed to offer physics, chemistry and biology courses, courses in integrated science are also found to permeate secondary education. Such integrated science courses are offered by Malta even upto grade 11. Romania also offers integrated science in grade 9 to 12.

Separate courses in all three sciences – biology, chemistry and physics are to be found in almost every country. Apart from these traditional science subjects taught in secondary school, some countries offer 1 year course in astronomy, geology and other subjects. German Democratic republic offers astronomy in grade 10. In Greece, geology is offered in grade 10 and cosmology in grade 11. In Spain geology is offered in grade 12 and in Portugal, ecology is offered in grade 10.

CHAPTER 3

Methods of Teaching Science

3.1 INTRODUCTION

By teaching science we aim at bringing about a desirable behavioural changes among pupils. Teaching is thus a most difficult task and every body is not fit to be a teacher. Some persons may have a 'flair' for teaching and such persons have the ability to awaken interest and arrest the attention of the students. Some others who are not so fortunate can improve their teaching through practice if they are fully acquainted with various methods of teaching. In order to make children learn effectively, the teacher has to adopt the right method of teaching. For choosing right method for a given situation the teacher must be familiar with different methods of teaching. In this chapter an effort will be made to discuss common methods used for teaching of science.

3.2 VARIOUS METHODS OF TEACHING SCIENCE

1. Lecture Method

Lecture method is the most commonly used method of teaching science. This method is most commonly followed in colleges and in schools in big classes. This method is not quite suitable to realise the real aim of teaching science. In lecture method only the teacher talks and students are passive listners. Since the students do not actively participate in this method of teaching so this method is a teacher controlled and information centred and in this method teacher works as a sole resource in class room instructions. Due to lack of participation students get bored and some of them some times may go to sleep. In this method students is provided with readymade knowledge by the teacher and due to this spoon feeding the students loses interest and his powers of reasoning and observation get no stimulus.

In this method the teacher goes ahead with the subject matter at his own speed. The teacher may make use of black board at times and may also dictate notes. This teacher oriented method in its extreme from does not expect any question or response from the students.

Advantages of Lecture Method

It has the following advantages:

(*i*) It is quite economical method. It is possible to handle a large number of students at a time and no laboratory, equipment, aids, materials are required.

(*ii*) Using this method the knowledge can be imparted to the students quickly and the prescribed syllabus can be covered in a short time.

(*iii*) It is quite attractive and easy to follow. Using this method teacher feels secure and satisfied.

(*iv*) It simplifies the task of the teacher as he dominates the lesson for 70-85% of the lesson time and students just listen to him.

(*v*) Using this method it is quite easy to impart factual information and historical anecdotes.

(*vi*) By following this method teacher can develop his own style of teaching and exposition.

(*vii*) In this method teacher can easily maintain the logical sequence of the subject by planning his lectures in advance. It minimises the chances of any gaps or overlappings.

(*viii*) Some good lectures delivered by the teacher may motivate, instigate, inspire a student for some creative thinking.

Disadvantages of Lecture Method

The disadvantages of lecture method can be as under:

(*i*) In this method the students participation is negligible and students become passive recipients of information.

(*ii*) In this method we are never sure if the students are concentrating and understanding the subject matter being taught to them by the teacher.

(*iii*) In this method knowledge is imparted so rapidly that weak students develop a hatred for learning.

(*iv*) It does not allow all the faculties of the student to develop.

(*v*) In this method there is no place of 'learning by doing' and thus teaching by this method strikes at the very root of science.

(*vi*) It does not take into account the previous knowledge of the student.

(*vii*) It does not provide for corrective feed back and remedial help to slow learners.

(*viii*) It does not cater to the individual needs and differences of students.

(*ix*) It does not help to inculcate scientific attitudes and training in scientific method among the pupils.

(*x*) It is an undemocratic and authoritarian method in which students depend only as the authority of the teacher. They cannot challange or question the verdict of the teacher. This checks the development of power of critical thinking and proper reasoning in the student.

Conclusion

After considering various merits and demerits of method it may be concluded that this method may be suitable for teaching in higher classes (XI, XII) where we aim to cover the prescribed syllabus quickly. In these classes this method can be used successfully for imparting factual knowledge, introducing some new and difficult topics, make generalisation from the facts already known to the students, revision of lessons already learnt etc.

Teaching by this method these students of classes XI and XII will also help those students who intend to join college so that they can prepare themselves for college where lecture method of teaching is a dominant method of imparting instruction.

This method of teaching can be made more beneficial if the teacher encourages his students to take notes during the lesson. After the lesson teacher can give his students some time for asking questions and answer their queries without any hesitation. While delivering his lesson the teacher may see that the lesson is delivered in good tone, loudly and clearly. He should use only simple and understandable words for delivering his lesson. If a teacher can introduce some humour in his lesson it would keep students interested in his lesson.

2. Lecture Demonstration Method

This method of teaching is sometimes also referred to as *Lecture-cum Demonstration Method*. This is considered to be a superior method of teaching in comparison to lecture method. In lecture method the teacher speaks and students listen so it is a one way traffic of flow of ideas and students are only passive listeners. This one sidedness is the major drawback of lecture method. A teaching method is considered better if both teacher and taught are active participants in the process of teaching. This particular aspect is taken care of in demonstration method.

This lecture-demonstration method is used by good science teachers for imparting science education in class room. By using this method it is possible to easily impart concrete experiences to students during the course of a lesson when the teacher wants to explain some abstract points. This method combines the instructional strategy of 'information imparting' and 'showing how'. This method combines the advantages of both the lecture method and the demonstration method.

In this method of teaching the teacher performs experiment before the class and simultaneously explains what he is doing. He also asks relevant questions from the class and students are compelled to observe carefully because they have to describe each and every step of the experiment accurately and draw inferences. After thorough questioning and cross-questioning the inferences drawn by the students are discussed in the class. In this way the students remain active participants in the process of teaching. The teacher also relates the outcomes of his experiment to the content of the on-going lesson. Thus while in lecture method teacher merely talks in demonstration method he really teaches.

Principle

This method is based on the principle: *Truth is that which works*.

Requirements for a Good Demonstration

For success of any demonstration following points be always kept in mind:

(*i*) It should be planned and rehearsed by the teacher before hand.

(*ii*) The apparatus used for demonstration should be big enough to be seen by the whole class. It would be much better if a large mirror is placed at a suitable angle above the teachers table which will enable the pupils to have a view of everything that the teacher is doing while performing the experiment.
Alternately, if the class is well disciplined the teacher may allow the students to sit on the stools placed on the benches to enable them to have a better view.

(*iii*) Adequate lighting arrangements be made on demonstration table and a proper back ground be provided.

(*iv*) All the pieces of apparatus be placed in order before starting the demonstration. The apparatus likely to be used should be placed on the left hand side of the table and it should be arranged in the same order in which it is likely to be used. After an apparatus is used it should be transferred to right hand side. Only things relevant to the lesson be placed on demonstration table.

(*v*) Before actually starting the demonstration, a clear statement about the purpose of demonstration be made to the students.

(*vi*) The teacher must make sure that the demonstration-cum-lecture method leads to active participation of the students in the process of learning. This he can achieve by putting well structured questions.

(*vii*) The demonstration should be quick and slick and should not appear to linger on unnecessarily.

(*viii*) The demonstration should be interesting so that it captures the attention of the students.

(*ix*) The teacher must be sure of success of the experiment to be demonstrated and for this he should rehears the experiment under the conditions prevailing in the class room. However even after all the necessary precaution the experiment fails in the class room due to one reason or the other, the teacher should not get nervous instead he should make an effort to find the reasons for the failure of the experiment. Sometimes in this process a good teacher may draw very useful conclusions.

(*x*) No complaints about inadequate and faulty apparatus he made by the teacher. In such a situation a good teacher finds an opportunity to show his skill.

(*xi*) It would be much better if the teacher demonstrates those experiments which are connected with common things which are seen and handled by students in their every day life.

(*xii*) There should be a correlation between the demonstrations and the sequence of experiments performed by the students in their practical classes.

(*xiii*) For active participation of students, the teacher may call individual student, in turn, to help him in demonstration work.

(*xiv*) During lecture-cum-demonstration session, teacher must act like a 'showman' and a 'performer'. He should know different ways of arresting the attention of the students.

(*xv*) He should write, a summary of the principles arrived at because of demonstration, on the black board. The black board can also be used for drawing necessary diagrams.

How to Conduct a Demonstration Lesson

We commonly find science teachers making use of demonstration method for teaching of science. The conduct of a demonstration lesson is very difficult and here we will try to discuss some of the essential steps that should be followed in a demonstration lesson.

1. *Planning and Preparation*

A great care be taken by the teacher while planning and preparing his demonstration lesson. He should keep the following points in mind while preparing his lesson:

(a) subject matter,

(b) questions to be asked;

(c) apparatus required for the experiment

To achieve the above stated objective the teacher should thoroughly go through the pages of the text book, relevant to the lesson. After this he should prepare his lesson plan in which he should essentially include the principles to be explained, a list of experiments to be demonstrated and the type of questions to be asked from the students. These questions be arranged in a systematic order that has to be followed in the class. Before actually demonstrating the experiment to a class the experiment be rehearsed under the conditions prevailing in the class room. Inspite of this, some thing may go wrong at the actual lesson, so reserve apparatus is often useful. The apparatus should be arranged in a systematic order on the demonstration table. Thus for the success of demonstration method a teacher has to prepare himself as thoroughly as a bride prepares herself for the marriage.

2. *Introduction of the Lesson*

As in every other subject so also in case of science the lesson should start with proper motivation of the students. It is always considered more useful to introduce the lesson in a problematic way which would make students realise the importance of the topic. The usual ways in which a teachers could easily introduce his lesson is by telling some personal experience or incident a simple and interesting experiment, a familiar ancedote or by telling a story.

A good experiment when carefully demonstrated is likely to leave an everlasting impression on the young mind of the pupil and it would set his pupils talking in school and out of it, about the interesting experiment that had been demonstrated to them in the science class. This should be kept in mind not only to start the lesson but be used, on every suitable occasion, during the lesson.

It is not possible to give an exhaustive list of such interesting experiments but as an illustration we can consider the opening of soda water bottle in the class room, by the teacher, following by a direct question to his pupil, have they seen any gas coming out of the bottle? At this stage the teacher can introduce the topic of carbon dioxide. Similarly a lesson on magnet and magnetism may be introduced by telling the story of the shephered boy and his crook. The simple way to introduce a lesson about human heart is to prick in the finger of one of the students which will result in blood coming out. The teacher can now introduce the lesson by asking the question, from where has this blood come?

3. *Presentation*

The method of presenting the subject matter is very important. A good teacher should present his lesson in an interesting manner and not in a boring way. To make the lesson interesting the teacher may not be very rigid to remain within the prescribed course rather he should make the lesson as much broad based as is possible. For widening of his lesson the teacher may think of various useful applications of the principle taught by him. He is also at liberty to take examples and illustrations from other allied branches of science to make his lesson interesting. The life history and some interesting facts from the life of the great scientist whose name is associated with the topic under discussion can also be cited to make the lesson interesting. Thus every effort be made to present the matter in a lively and interesting manner and a lesson should never be presented as 'dry bones' of an academic course. Thus in a lesson dealing with Archimedes principle the teacher should not feel satisfied just by stating the principle and then demonstrating it with one or two experiments rather he should discuss its applications in daily life such as ships, floating bodies, diving and rising of submarines, the use of balloons and air ships etc. It is also advisable to make use of pictures, posters, diagrams, slides, films etc. in addition to experiments to illustrate the topic in hand.

Constant questions and answers should from part of every demonstration lesson. Questions and cross questions are essential for properly illuminating the principle being discussed. Questions be arranged in such a way that their answers from a complete teaching unit. Though an effort be made to encourage the students to answer a large number of questions but if students fails to answer some questions teacher should provide the answers to such questions. It is unwise to expect all the answers from the pupil and a teacher should feel satisfied if he has been able to create a desire in a student to know what he does not know.

The lesson the presented in a clear voice and the teacher should speak slowly and with correct pronunciation. He should avoid the use of any bombastic and ambiguous terms. The continuous talk is likely to monotony and to avoid it experiments be well spaced throughout the lesson.

4. *Performance of Experiments*

A good observer has been described as a person who has learned to use his senses of touch, sight, smell and hearing in an intelligent and alert manner. We want children to observe what happens in experiments and to have ample opportunities to state their observations carefully. We also want them to try to explain what happens in reference to their problem, but we want to make certain. There is separation between observations and generalization and conclusions. We will be violating the true spirit of science if we allow children to generalise from one experiment or observation.

The following steps are generally accepted as valuable in developing and concluding science experiments with the children;

1. Write the problems to be solved in simple words so that every one understands.
2. Make a list of activities that will be used to solve problems.
3. Gather material for conducting experiments.
4. Work out a format of the steps in the order of procedure so that every one knows what is to be done.
5. The teacher should always try the experiment himself to become acquainted with the equipment and procedure.
6. Record the findings in ways commensurate with the maturity level and purposes of the student.
7. Assist students in making generalisations from conclusions only after sufficient evidence and experiences.

The demonstration experiment be presented by the teacher in a model way. He should work in a tidy, clean and orderly manner while demonstrating an experiment. Some of the important points to be kept in mind while demonstrating an experiment are as under:

(*i*) Experiments should be simple and speedy
(*ii*) The experiments must work and their results should be clear and striking.
(*iii*) Experiments be properly spaced throughout the lesson.
(*iv*) Keep some reserve apparatus on the demonstration table.

(*v*) Keep the demonstration apparatus in tact till it has to be used again.

5. *Black Board Summary*

A summary of important results and principles be written on the black board. Use of black board should also be frequently made for drawing necessary sketches and diagrams. The black board summary should be written in neat, clean and legible way. Since black board summary is an index to a teacher's ability he should keep the following points in mind while writing on black board.

(*i*) Proper space be left between different letters and words.

(*ii*) Always start writing from left hand corner of the black board.

(*iii*) Start a new line only when the first one has extended across the black board.

(*iv*) Take care not to divide the words at the end of a time.

(*v*) Make all efforts to keep all the paragraphs and similar signs in calculations under one another.

(*vi*) While drawing sketches and diagrams preferably use 'single lined' diagrams.

(*vii*) All the diagrams drawn on the board be properly labelled.

6. *Supervision*

Students be asked to take the complete notes of the black board summary including the sketches and diagrams drawn. Such a record will be quite helpful to the student for learning his lesson. Such a summary will prove beneficial only if it has been copied correctly from the black board and to make sure that students are copying the black board summary properly the teacher should check it by frequently going to the seats of the students.

Common Errors in a Demonstration Lesson

A summary of common errors committed while delivering a demonstration lesson is given below:

(*i*) The apparatus may not be ready for use

(*ii*) There may not be an apparent relation between the demonstration experiment and the topic under discussion.

(*iii*) Black board summary is not upto the mark.

(*iv*) Teacher may be in a hurry to arrive at generalisation without allowing sufficient time to arrive at these generalisation from facts.

(*v*) Teacher may some times fail to ask right type of questions.

(*vi*) Teacher some times may use a difficult language.

(*vii*) Teacher some times takes to talking more which may mar the enthusiasm of the students.

(*viii*) Teacher may not have allowed sufficient time for recording data etc.

(*ix*) Teacher has not given proper attention to supervision.

Merits of Demonstration Method

Following are the merits of this method

(*i*) It is an economical method as compared to purely student centred approaches.

(*ii*) It is a psychological method and students take active interest in teaching learning process.

(*iii*) It leads students from concrete to abstract situations and thus is more psychological.

(*iv*) It is a suitable method if the apparatus to be handled is costly and sensitive. Such an apparatus is likely to damaged if handled by students.

(*v*) This method can be more safe if the experiments to be demonstrated are dangerous.

(*vi*) In comparison to Heuristic method, project etc., it is time saving but lecture method is too speedy.

(*vii*) It can be used successfully for all types of students.

(*viii*) In this method such experiments which are difficult for students can be included.

(*ix*) This method can be used to impart manual and manipulative skills to students.

Disadvantages of Demonstration Method

Some of the disadvantages of this method are as under:

(*i*) It provides no scope for 'learning by doing' for students as students just observe what the teacher is performing. Thus students fail to relish the joys of direct personal experience.

(*ii*) Since the teacher performs the experiment in his own pace, many students cannot comprehend the concept being clarified.

(*iii*) Since the method is not child centred so it makes no provision for individual differences. All types of students including slow learners and genius have to proceed with the same speed.

(*iv*) It fails to develop laboratory skills in the students. It can not work as a substitute for laboratory work by students in which they are required to handle the apparatus themselves.

(*v*) It fails to impart training in scientific attitude.

(*vi*) In this method students many a times fail to observe many finer details of the apparatus used because they observe it from a distance.

Conclusion

It is thoroughly accepted that success is greater with experiments in elementary schools if they start with a real purpose, are simply done with uncomplicated apparatus, are done by children under careful direction of the teacher, and help the children think and draw valid, tentative conclusion.

This is considered as one of the best methods of teaching science to secondary classes. An effort be made to involve a larger number of students by calling them in batches to the demonstration table.

Science teachers should encourage more direct experimentation by children in order to help children broaden their range of fact finding skills beyond three T's – teacher, textbook, television.

3. Heuristic Method

Heuristic method is a pure discovery method of learning science independent of teacher. The writings and teachings of H.E. Armstrong, Professor of Chemistry at the City and Guilds Institute, London, have had much influence in promoting since teaching in schools. He was a strong advocate of a special type of laboratory training – heuristic training ('heuristic' is derived from the Greek word meaning 'to discover'). In Heuristic method, the student be put in the place of an independent discoverer. Thus no help or guidance is provided by the teacher in this method. In this method the teacher sets a problem for the students and then stands aside while they discover the answer.

In words of Professor Armstrong, "Heuristic methods of teaching are methods which involve our placing students as far as possible in the attitude of the discoverer – methods which involve their finding out instead of being merely told about things".

The method requires the student to solve a number of problems experimentally. To almost every one – especially children – experiments and science are synonymous. Once an idea occurs to a scientist he immediately thinks in terms of ways of trying out his ideas to see if he is correct. Trying to confirm or disprove some thing, or simply to test an idea, is the backbone of the experiment. Experiments start with questions in order to find answers, solve problems, clarify ideas or just to see what happens. Experimenting should be part of the elementary school science programme as an aid to helping children find solutions to science problems as well as for helping them to develop appreciation for one of the basic tools of science.

Procedure of the Method

The method requires the students to solve a number of problems experimentally. Each student is required to discover everything for himself and is to be told nothing. The students are led to discover facts with the help of experiments, apparatus and books. In this method the child behaves like a research scholar.

In the stage managed heuristic method, a problem sheet with minimum instructions is given to the student and he is required to perform the experiments concerning the problem in hand. He must follow the instructions, and enter in his notebook an account of what he has done and results arrived at. He must also put down his conclusion as to the bearing which the result has on the problem in hand. In this way he is led to reason from observation.

Essentially therefore, the heuristic method is intended to provide a training in method. Knowledge is a secondary consideration altogether. The method is formative rather than informational.

The procedures and skills in science problem solving can only be developed in class rooms where searching is encouraged, creative thinking is respected, and where it is safe to investigate, try out ideas, and even make mistakes.

Teachers Attitudes

One of the most important aspects of the problem solving approach to children's development in scientific thinking is the teachers attitude. His approach should be teaching science with a question mark instead of with an exclamation point. The acceptance of and the quest for unique solutions for the problem that the class is investigating should be a guiding principle in the teacher's approach to his programme of science. Teachers must develop sensitiveness to children and to the meanings of their behaviour. Teachers should be ready to accept any suggestion for the solution of problems regardless of how irrelevant it may seem to him, for this is really the true spirit of scientific problem solving. By testing various ideas it can be shown to the child that perhaps his suggestion was not in accord with the information available. It can then be shown that this failure gets us much closer to the correct solution by eliminating one possibility from many offered by the problem.

In this method teacher should avoid the tempetation to tell the right answer to save time. The teacher should be convinced that road to scientific thinking takes time. Children should never be exposed to ridicule for their suggestions of possible answers otherwise they will show a strong tendency to stop suggestions.

For success of this method a teacher should act like a guide and should provide only that much guidance as is rightly needed by the student. He should be sympathetic and courteous and should be capable enough to plan and devise problems for investigation by pupils. He should be capable of good supervision and be able to train the pupils in a way that he himself becomes dispensable.

Merits of Heuristic Method

This method of teaching science has the following merits:

(*i*) It develops the habit of enquiry and investigation among students.

(*ii*) It develops habit of self learning and self direction.

(*iii*) It develops scientific attitudes among students by making them truthful and honest for they learn how to arrive at decisions by actual experimentations.

(*iv*) It is psychologically sound system of learning as it is based on the maximum, "learning by doing".

(*v*) It develops in the student a habit of diligency.

(*vi*) In this method most of the work is done in school and so the teacher has no worry to assign on check home task.

(*vii*) It provides scope for individual attention to be paid by the teacher and for closer contacts. These contacts help in establishing cordial relations between the teacher and the taught.

Limitations of Heuristic Method

Main limitations of this method are as under:

(*i*) It is a long and time consuming method and so it becomes difficult to cover the prescribed syllabus in time.

(*ii*) It pre-supposes a very small class and a gifted teacher and the method is too technical and scientific to be handled by an average teacher. The method expects of the teacher a great efficiency and hard work, experience and training.

(*iii*) There is a tendency on the part of the teacher to emphasize those branches and parts of the subject which lend themselves to heuristic treatment and to ignore important branches of the subject which do not involve measurement and quantitative work and are therefore not so suitable.

(*iv*) It is not suitable for beginners. In the early stages, the students needs enough guidance which if not given, may greatly disappoint them and it is possible that the child may develop a distaste for studies.

(*v*) In this method too much stress is placed on practical work which may lead a student to form a wrong idea of the nature of science as a whole. They grow up in the belief that science is some thing to be done in the laboratory, forgetting that laboratories were made for science and not science for laboratories.

(*vi*) The gradation of problems is a difficult task which requires sufficient skill and training. The succession of exercises is rarely planned to fit into a general scheme for building up the subject completely.

(*vii*) Some times experiments are performed merely for sake of doing them.

(*viii*) Learning by this method, pupils leave school with little or no scientific appreciation of their physical environment. The romance of modern scientific discovery and invention remains out of picture for them and the humanizing influence of the subject has been kept away from them.

(*ix*) Evaluation of learning through heuristic method can be quite tedious.

(*x*) Presently enough teachers are not available for implementing learning by heuristic method.

Conclusion

This method cannot be successfully applied in primary classes but this method can be given a trial in secondary classes particularly in higher secondary classes. However, in the absence of gifted teachers, well equipped laboratories and libraries and other limitations this method has not been given a trial in our schools. Even if these limitations are removed this method may not prove much useful under the existing circumstances and prevailing rules and regulations. Though not recommending the use of heuristic method for teaching of science it may be suggested that at least a heuristic approach prevails for teaching of science in our schools. By heuristic approach we mean that students be not spoon fed or be given a dictation rather they be given opportunities to investigate, to think and work independently alongwith traditional way of teaching.

4. Assignment Method

The heuristic method is based exclusively on laboratory work where as the lecture method and demonstration method do not give any opportunity for laboratory work. For teaching of science, assignment method is best suited because it involves a harmonious combination of training at the demonstration table and individual laboratory work. In this method of teaching science, the given syllabus is split into well planned assignments with a set of instructions about solving the assignments. It is also possible to plan assignments based on the individual needs of the students.

Procedure

The whole of the prescribed course is divided into so many connected weekly portion or assignments. One topic is taken and a set of instructions regarding the study is drawn up. The printed page containing instructions or the assignment is handed to the pupil a week in advance of their practical work. They are then required to read the pages of the text book referred to in the assignment and write answers to a few (generally not more than three or four) questions in a note-book. The students then hand over these answers to the teacher a day before the practicals. The teacher corrects the answers. If there are a lot of mistakes in the assignments then the teacher sets the remedial and corrective assignments.

The second part of every assignment consists of laboratory work. Full instructions about laboratory work *i.e.* fitting up of apparatus, recording of results, precautions to be taken etc. On the day of the practical work the students are returned their note-books and those students whose preparatory work is found satisfactory by the teacher are allowed to proceed with the practical work.

Teaching by this method demands a lot of careful planning by the teacher and generally two out of six periods allotted to science in time-table are reserved for demonstration work and remaining four for practical work. During periods reserued for demonstration work teacher gives a demonstration on a topic that is considered to be a difficult one by the pupils. These period can also be utilized by the teacher to clarify some facts which are not very clear to the pupils. For the success of assignment method the teacher should prepare a list of experiments to be demonstrated by him and another list of experiments which are to be done by the students. The success of this method mainly depends on properly drawn assignments. If the teacher keeps a progress chart he can easily distinguish between a good and an average or dull student. He can then prepare special assignments according to the needs of the student. An assign- ment chart may be of the following type:

Assignment Method

Specimen of Progress Chart

School ______ Class ______ From ______ To ______

No.	*Name of Student*	*Class Test Result*					*Assignments*					*Term Exam. Results*			*Remarks*
		1	*2*	*3*	*4*	......	*1*	*2*	*3*	*4*	......	*I*	*II*	*III*	

Aims

Aims of assignment method are as follows:

(*i*) To provide a synthesis of various methods of learning.

(*ii*) To provide students a training in information processing.

(*iii*) To develop a habit of self study among the students.

(*iv*) To develop scientific attitude and a habit of critical thinking among students.

(*v*) To expose students to various resources of leaning.

To achieve these aims the following points be kept in mind while drawing up an assignment.

(*i*) The assignment must be based on one textbook.

(*ii*) The assignment should clearly state what portion of textbook are to be read.

(*iii*) It should draw attention to particular points and give explanation of difficult points.

(*iv*) It should also indicate those portions of matter which can be omitted by the students.

(*v*) Questions are an essential part of the assignment and the questions be so designed that

(*a*) they test whether the student has read and understood the portion assigned.

(*b*) their answers are short.

(*c*) their answers require diagrams to be drawn

(*d*) they ask for a list of apparatus for coming laboratory work

(*vi*) In each assignment the teacher should indicate portion of book dealing with the same or allied topics.

(*vii*) The assignment should include detailed instructions about the experiment. This portion of instructions should include.

(*a*) the procedure of the experiment.

(*b*) the method of recording results.

(*c*) the precautions to be observed.

(*d*) a diagram illustrating the set up of the apparatus.

Features of a Good Assignment

(*i*) It should be related to subject matter under study.

(*ii*) It should be concise and balanced which can be finished by student easily and quickly.

(*iii*) Its purpose should be clear and its objective be made known to the students.

(*iv*) It should be so worded that it fosters thinking and independent learning.

(*v*) It should be such so as to suit to the age, aptitudes and interest of the student.

(*vi*) It should be able to combine various methods of teaching.

Teacher's Role

The teacher has to do the following for the success of assignment method of teaching.

(*i*) He should split up the prescribed course in science into successive and progressive assignments.

(*ii*) He should list down the objectives for each assignment which students must achieve.

(*iii*) He should prepare a progress chart for each student.

(*iv*) He must prepare and provide a list of reference material required for each assignment.

(*v*) To cover up the learning gaps he should prepare remedial assignments.

(*vi*) He should also prepare activity sheets for laboratory work and experiments.

Merits of Assignment Method

This method of teaching has the following advantages

(*i*) It provides the students an opportunity for self study.

(*ii*) It synthesizes various methods of teaching of science and makes the learning process very effective.

(*iii*) It provides an opportunity to the student to learn at his own pace and thus the progress of the brighter students is not hindered by weaker students.

(*iv*) In this system teacher gets the central role of contingency manager and facilitator of learning. The teacher acts as a guide and interferes least in the student's work.

(*v*) It places more emphasis on practical work and provides students a training in skill of information processing.

(*vi*) It provides a feel for the scientific methods to students.

(*vii*) In this process the learning process can be individualized to a great extent by having differential assignment.

(*viii*) It provides for corrective feed back and remediation.

(*ix*) The progress chart with the teacher shows the progress of each student at a glance which gives the teacher an idea of a gifted and weaker students.

(*x*) In this process the student learns to work himself because in laboratory he is not provided with any laboratory attendant.

(*xi*) Habit of extra study is developed because a number of books for extra study are recommended by the teacher. Such a study helps in widening the outlook of the pupil.

(*xii*) Since the burden of work lies on pupil so he learns to take responsibility.

(*xiii*) Since the students perform experiments at their own speed so owing to their different speeds they do not perform the same experiment at the same time. Thus a large quantity of same kind of apparatus is not required.

Disadvantages of Assignment Method

Some of the disadvantages of assignment methods are as follows:

(*i*) It burdens the teacher with a lot of planning and thus increases his work load to a large extent. It requires the teacher to prepare a well thought out scheme for the year before starting the method.

(*ii*) No source material is available in the market for assignments preparation of assignments for different students becomes an uphill task for the teacher. For teaching science beginner is advised to use the book "Assignments in Practical Elementary Science" by Dr. Whitehouse. However, if a book other than "Experimental Science" by Gregory and Hodges is being used as a textbook then the above book of assignments should only be used after making necessary alteration in connection with references.

(*iii*) The success of method depends on the availability of rich library and laboratory facilities. It makes the method very expensive.

(*iv*) Before starting with this method teacher must satisfy himself that the apparatus and chemicals required for practical work are available in the laboratory. He should also satisfy himself about the availability of text books, laboratory manual, note book etc. and see that each student possesses them.

(*v*) Teacher should also be vigilant to see that weak students do not get a chance to copy the answers from the note books of brighter students.

(*vi*) Weaker students need a lot of help and guidance at individual level and it becomes an unnecessary drain on the teacher's energies.

(*vii*) This method is suitable only for a small graph of students.

Conclusion

Though the method has some limitations but can be used successfully if following points are given due consideration.

(*i*) The teacher should prepare a well thought out plan for the year.

(*ii*) He should find some good resource book and use the same after necessary changes.

(*iii*) He should be very particular to check copying by weaker students. As remedial measures the teacher should clearly explain difficult topics and principles to the students during demonstration class and set only a limited number of questions in his assignment.

(*iv*) The availability of apparatus and chemicals needed for experiment be confirmed before hand.

(*v*) Only those students who have. text book, laboratory mannual and note book whose preparatory work has been found to be satisfactory be allowed to do the practical work.

(*vi*) A new experiment be allowed to a student when he has completed his previous experiment and has shown it to the teacher.

(*vii*) Students be asked to record all their observations directly in the fair note book. They should be asked to complete their practical note book in the class itself.

(*viii*) Teacher can provide necessary help to needy students and for this he should move from one table to another when the students are performing the experiment.

5. Project Method

This method was given by Dewey—the American philosopher, psychologist and practical teacher. The project method is a direct outcome of his philosophy. According to Dr. Kilpatrick "A project is a unit of whole hearted purposeful activity carried on preferably, in its natural setting". According to Stevenson "A project is a problematic act carried to its completion in its natural setting". According to Ballard, "A project is a bit of real life that has been incorporated into the school".

The project method is not totally new. Project equivalents are advocated for the adolescent period by Rousseau in Emile (BK-III). A project plan is a modified form of an old method called "concentration-of-studies". The main features of "concentration-of-studies plan" is that some subject is taken as the core or centre and all other school subjects as they arise are studied in connection with it.

Project method is based on the following principles:

(*i*) Learning by doing.

(*ii*) Learning by living.

(*iii*) Children learn better through association, cooperation and activity.

What is an Educational Project?

Various definition of project has already been considered. A modified definition of project is given by Tomas and Long. They define it as "a voluntary undertaking which involves constructive effort or thought and eventuates into objective results".

Considering various definitions of project we may consider it as a kind of life experience which is an outcome of a craving or desire of the pupils. This is a method of spontaneous and incidental teaching. "Learning by living" may be a better meaning of project method, because life is full of projects and individuals carry out these projects in their every day life.

The projects may broadly be classified as

(*i*) Individual projects, and

(*ii*) Social projects

Individual projects are to be carried out by individuals where as social projects are carried out by a grant of individuals.

Steps in a Project

For completing a project we have five stages in actual practice. These are

(*i*) Providing a situation

(*ii*) Choosing and proposing.

(*iii*) Planning of the project.

(*iv*) Executing the project.

(*v*) Judging the project.

Recording the project is also essential.

(*i*) *Providing a Situation*

A project should arise out of a need felt by pupils and it should never be forced on them. It should be purposeful and significant. It should look important and must be interesting. For this the teacher should always be on the look out to find situation that arise and discuss them with students to discover their interests. Situations may be provided by different methods. Some such methods may include talking to students on the topics of common interest e.g. how did they spend their holidays, what did they see in Delhi etc.

(*ii*) *Choosing and Proposing*

From various definition of an educational project we get the same underlying ideas (*a*) school tasks are to be as real and as purposeful as the tasks of wider life beyond the school walls (*b*) they are of such a nature that the pupil is genuinely eager to carry them out in order to achieve a desirable and clearly realised aim.

According to Kilpatrick, "the part of the pupil and the part of the teacher, in most of the school work, depends largely on who does the proposing". The teacher should refrain from proposing any project otherwise the whole purpose of the method would be defeated. Teacher should only tempt the students for a particular project by providing a situation but the proposal for the project should finally come from students. The teacher must exercise guidance in selection of the project and if the students make an unwise choice, the teacher should tactfully guide them for a better project. The essentially of a good project are:

(*i*) It should have evident worth for the individual or the graph that undertakes them.

(*ii*) The project must have a bearing on a great number of subjects and the knowledge acquired through it may be applicable in a variety of ways.

(*iii*) The project should be timely.

(*iv*) The project should be challenging.

(*v*) The project should be feasible.

It is for the teacher to see that the purpose of the project is clearly defined and understood.

(iii) Planning

The students be encouraged by the teacher to plan out the details of the project. In the process of planning teacher has to act only as a guide and he should give suggestions at times but actual planning be left to the students.

(iv) Execution

Once the project has been chosen and the details of the project have been planned, the teacher should help the students in executing the project according to the plan. Since execution of a project is the longest step in the project method so it need a lot a patience on the part of the students and the teacher. During this step the teacher should carefully supervise the pupils in manipulative skills to prevent waste of materials and to guard accidents. The teacher should assign work to different students in accordance with their tastes, interests, aptitudes and capabilities. Teacher should see that every member of the grasp gets a chance to do some thing. Teacher should constantly check up the relation between the chalked out plans and the developing project and as far as possible 'at the spot' changes and modification be avoided. However if such changes become unavoidable these should be noted and reasons explained for future guidance.

(*v*) *Evaluation*

The evaluation of the project should be done both by the pupils and the teacher. The pupils should estimate the qualities of what they have done before the teacher gives his evaluation. The evaluation of the project has to be done in the light of plans, difficulties in the execution and achieved results. Let the students have self criticism and look through their own failings and findings. This step is very useful because as a result of the project, the pupils can know the values of the information, interest, skills and attitudes that have been modified by the project.

(*vi*) *Record*

A complete record of the project be kept by the students. The record should include every thing about the project. It should include the proposal, plan and its discussion, duties allotted to different students and how far were they carried out by them. It should also include the details of places visited and surveyed, maps etc. drawn, guidance for future and all other possible details.

Role of Teacher

(*i*) In project method of teaching the role of a teacher is that of a guide, friend and philosopher.

(*ii*) He helps the students in solving their problems just like an elder brother.

(*iii*) He encourages his students to work collectively, amicably in the graph.

(*iv*) He also helps his students to avoid mistakes.

(*v*) He makes it a point that each member of the group contributes some thing to the completion of the project and in this process helps the shy and weaker students to work along with their class mates.

(*vi*) If the students face failure during execution of some steps of the project the teacher should not execute any portion of the project but should only explain to his students the reasons of their failure and should suggest them some better methods or techniques that may be used by them next time for the success of the project

(*vii*) During the execution step teacher also learns some thing.

(*viii*) Teacher should always remain alert and active during execution, step and see that the project goes to completion successfully.

(*ix*) During execution of the project teacher should maintain a democratic atmosphere.

(*x*) Teacher must be well read and well informed so that he can help the students to the successful completion of the project.

Merits of the Project Method

(*i*) It is a method of teaching based on psychological laws of learning. The education is related to child's life and he acquires it through meaningful activity.

(*ii*) It imbibes the spirit of cooperation as it is a cooperative venture. Teacher and students join in the project.

(*iii*) It stimulates interest in natural as also man made situations. More over the interest is spontaneous and not under any compulsions.

(*iv*) The method provides opportunities for pupils of different tastes and aptitudes with in the frame work of the same scheme.

(*v*) It upholds the dignity of labour.

(*vi*) It introduces democracy in education.

(*vii*) It brings about a close correlation between a particular activity and various subjects.

(*viii*) It is a problem solving method and places very less emphasis on cramming or memorising.

(*ix*) It helps to inculcate social discipline through joint activities of the teacher and the taught.

(*x*) A project can be used to arouse interest in a particular topic as it blends school life with outside world. It provides situations in which the students come in direct contact with their environment.

(*xi*) It develops self confidence and self discipline.

(*xii*) A project tends to illustrate the real nature of the subject.

(*xiii*) A project affords opportunity to develop keenness and accuracy of observation and produces a spirit of enquiry.

(*xiv*) It puts a challenge to the student and thus stimulates constructive and creative thinking.

(*xv*) It provides the students an opportunity for mutual exchange of ideas.

(*xvi*) This method helps the children to organise their knowledge.

Drawbacks of the Project Method

(*i*) Projects require a lot of time and this method can be used as a part of science work only.

(*ii*) Though the method provides the student superficial knowledge of so many things it provides insufficient knowledge of some fundamental principles.

(*iii*) In the project planning and execution of the project the teacher is required to put in much more work in comparison to other methods of teaching.

(*iv*) The teacher has been assumed as master of all subjects which is practically not possible.

(*v*) Good text books on these lines have not yet been produced.

(*vi*) It is an expensive method is it involves tours, excursions, purchase of apparatus and equipment etc.

(*vii*) The method of organising instructions is unsystematised and thus the regular time table of work will be upset.

(*viii*) The method may fit those who cannot listen but it is very questionable if it has the same value for those who can listen.

(*ix*) The method leaves a gap in pupils knowledge.

(*x*) It underestimates man's power of imagination which enables him to savour the full experience of another without the necessity of undergoing the experience himself.

(*xi*) Some times the projects may be too ambitious and beyond pupils capacity to accomplish.

(*xii*) Larger projects in hands of an unexperienced teacher lead to boredom.

(*xiii*) The education given by projects is likely to emphasise relationships in breadth than in depth.

Conclusion

The project method provides a practical approach to learning of both theoretical and practical problems. If it is difficult to follow this method of teaching it would be better at least not to ignore the spirit of this method.

This method has been found to be more suitable for primary and middle classes and is of restricted use for high and higher secondary classes. This method may be tried alongwith formal class room teaching without disturbing the school time-table. With this in view some projects may be undertaken by the students to be completed on certain fixed days of a week. Alternately first half of the day may be devoted to class room teaching and the project work be carried out in the remaining half day. To help solve the problem of fund's shortage such projects be choose which are self-supporting or the projects selected be such that their final products can be sold to partially support the funds. Some such projects are improvising science apparatus, growing a vegetable garden etc. Costly projects should be avoided. As it is not suitable for drill and continuous and systematic teaching, it is not very desirable to use it freely.

Some Projects for Science Class

Here are given some projects for a science class.

1. Our food
2. Our atmosphere
3. Water
4. Air.

6. Concentric Method

This is a system of organising a course rather than a method of teaching. It is therefore better to call it *concentric system* or *approach*. It implies widening of knowledge just as concentric circles go on extending and widening. It is a system of arrangement of subject matter. In this method the study of the topic is spread over a number of years. It is based on the principle that subject cannot be given an exhaustive treatment at the first stage. To begin with, a simple presentation of the subject is given and further knowledge is imparted in following years. Thus beginning from a nucleus the circles of knowledge go on widening year after year and hence the name concentric method.

Procedure

A topic is divided into a number of portions which are then allotted to different classes. The criterion for allotment of a particular portion of the course to a particular class are the difficulty of portion and power of comprehension of students in that age group. Thus it is mainly concerned with year to year teaching but its influence can also be exercised in day-to-day teaching. Knowledge be given today should follow from knowledge given yesterday and should lead to teaching on following day.

Merits of Concentric Method

(*i*) This method of organisation of subject matter is decidely superior to that in which one topic is taken up in particular class and an effort is made to deal with all aspects of the topic in that particular class.

(*ii*) In provides a frame work from science course which is of real value to students.

(*iii*) The system is most successful when the teaching is in hands of one teacher because then he can preserve continuity in the teaching and keeps his expanding circle concentric.

(*iv*) It provides opportunity for revision of work already covered in a previous class and carrying out new work.

(*v*) It enables the teacher to cover a portion according to receptivity of learner.

(*vi*) Since the same topic is learnt over many years so its impressions are more lasting.

(*vii*) It does not allow teaching to become dull because every year a new interest can be given to the topic. Every year there are new problems to solve and new difficulties to overcome.

Drawbacks

For the success of this approach we require really capable teacher. If a teacher becomes over ambitious and exhausts all the possible interesting illustrations in the introductory year then the subject loses its power of freshness and appeal and nothing is left to create interest in the topic in subsequent years.

In case the topic is too short or too long then also the method is not found to be useful. A too long portion makes the topic dull and a two short portion fails to leave any permanent and lasting impression on the mind of the pupil.

Conclusion

It is a good method for being adopted for arranging the subject matter. It should be kept in mind, by the organisers, while organising the subject matter that no portion is too long or too short. It would also be much useful if the same teacher teaches the same class year after year so that he can reserve some illustrative examples for each year and thus can maintain the interest of the students in the topic.

7. Unit Method

It is one of the latest methods in the field of education. It involves pupils more actively in learning process.

Different authors define *unit* in a different way. Hanna, Hageman, Potter define it as, "a unit is a purposeful learning experience that is focussed on some socially significant understanding which will modify the behaviour of learner and adjust him to adjust to a life situation more effectively".

However all the definitions of *unit* imply that it possesses the following characteristics.

(*i*) It is an organisation of activities around a purpose.

(*ii*) It has significant content.

(*iii*) It involves students in learning process.

(*iv*) It modifies the students behaviour to such an extent that he can cope with new problems and situations more competently.

Types of Units

Mainly the units may be classified as

(*i*) Subject matter units.

(*ii*) Experience units.

(*iii*) Resource units.

The teaching of general science can be carried out in a better way and it is better understood and appreciated by the students if it is taught as units of immediate interest to the pupils. Such units may be (*i*) life centred (*ii*) environment centred (*iii*) life and environment centred.

For this The Tara Devi Seminar[1] (1956) recommended the following:

Life Centred Units

1. The world that science has built.
2. The air we breathe.
3. The water we use.
4. The food we eat.
5. How man gets his food.
6. The clothes we wear.
7. The homes we live in.
8. The machines we use.
9. The power we work with.
10. Protection from disease.
11. Our biological resources.
12. Our mineral resources.

---

1. *Report of All India Seminar on the Teaching of Science in Secondary Schools, held at Tara Devi (Simla Hills), 1956, Ministry of Education, New Delhi.*

13. Means of transport.
14. Means of communicate with the world.
15. The universe we live in.
16. Story of life.
17. How to be yourself.

Environment-centred Units

1. The atmosphere.
2. Water, a vital need of life.
3. The earth surface.
4. Fire and heat.
5. Effects on heating and cooling in air and water.
6. Study of light.
7. Civilization and the use of metals.
8. Work and energy (the occupations of man).
9. Problems of transport and communication.
10. Plants and animals in relation to life.
11. The study of the body-machine.
12. Understanding ourselves.
13. Science and philosophy of life.

Environment of Life-centred Units

1. The world that science has built.
2. Your body-machine and how it works.
3. Health to you.
4. Using biological resources for better living.
5. Using mineral resources for better living.
6. Energy and machines for the world of tomorrow.
7. Time, measurement and mass production.
8. The weather and what we can do about it.
9. Astronomy;
   (a) The solar system in which we live.
   (b) Billions of stars and other universes.
10. Science for our homes.

For teaching science the lessions are grouped round the various topics. For learning a unit entitled 'means of transport' we can group the lessons dealing with various means of transport such as bicycle, steam engine, internal combustion engine, electric motor, aeroplanes, ships etc. While dealing with these we can introduces many ideas e.g. while teaching about bicycle we can introduce the study of levers, use of levers for harnessing energy, gaining speed with the help of livers etc. Some new term as speed, velocity, acceleration, retardation, brake, friction, lubrication, mechanical advantage etc. may also be introduced. While dealing with electric motors we can tell the use of such motors in electric trains, generation and transmission of electricity. The terms volt, ohm, resistance, capacitance etc. can also be introduced.

Similarly for teaching of biology 'Farm', 'Garden', 'Pond' etc. can be used as a unit. From it we can introduce the student to the teaching of various kind of soils, insects, water, weather etc.

Similar interesting lessons can be developed on 'Air', 'Water' etc. These can be used for teaching of hydrogen, nitrogen, water, carbon di-oxide etc.

Essentials of a Good Unit

(*i*) It should deal with a sizeable topic.

(*ii*) It should emerge out of students past experiences and should lead to broader interests.

(*iii*) It should be of appropriate difficulty in terms of child's understanding, interest.

(*iv*) It should provide scope for using a variety of materials and activities like community resources, audiovisual materials etc.

(*v*) It should allow use of sufficient amount of books and other learning materials.

(*vi*) Units should be such as to draw materials from several fields so that children may develop richer insight into human relationships and processes.

(*vii*) It should be functional and should be in accordance with the maturity level of the learner.

Merits of Unit Method

This method of teaching has the following advantages:

(*i*) It brings about a closer integration between various branches of science.

(*ii*) It makes subject matter more interesting and realistic.

(*iii*) It provides a better understanding of the environment and life.

(*iv*) It focuses attention on significant facts and avoids confusion.

(*v*) The unit because of its flexibility provides facility in adopting instructions to individual's differences.

(*vi*) It is quite useful to teaching general science in elementary classes.

Limitations of Unit Method

(*i*) This method cannot be used if the teacher is required to complete some prescribed course in a specified time.

(*ii*) There are only a few teachers who are so widely read that they can introduce material and illustration from various branches of science while keeping before their students one central topic.

Unit method or *topic method* is a varied slightly in America. In American schools the teacher announces one topic and the students are asked to say what they already know about it. Then the topic is discussed in a question and answer session and those questions which no member of the class could answer are noted down for investigation. From this list of questions, such questions as are considered as too difficult for a particular class are eliminated by the teacher and the remaining questions are arranged in a planned manner for answers. These questions are then dealt within the class according to the plan. The great thing about such a course is that boys feel that it is their course and not some thing thrust upon them by authority.

In some American schools the teacher announces a topic and then hands over to the class a piece of mechanism, say electric bell, and asks them to discover everything about it. He adverse them to consult books, to ask questions and then come prepared, for discussion with his, after a week.

8. Historical Method

Some teachers prefer to develop a subject by following the stages through which the subject has passed during its course of development from its early beginnings. This type of teaching has a fascination which appeals to pupils. Various science subjects such as Chemistry, Physics, Bacteriology etc. which have an interesting historical back- ground can be taught successfully by such a technique. It is possible to develop a topic starting from its early history and the various stages through which it developed before attaining the modern shape.

Chemistry, in particular, has a very interesting history and the works of Priestley, Lavoisier, Davy, Black and Dalton etc. can be given this type of treatment. The gradual development of atomic theory can be unfolded gradually by this method which will be quite interesting. Similarly the teacher can use stories from the history of science (e.g. Archimedes and his bath, Newton and the apple etc.) to arouse interest of the students in the topic under consideration.

While discussing the subject of Bacteriology the historical treatment can include invention and development of the microscope.

Through such a treatment may not be possible for all the topics but an occasional resort to such a treatment has its own uses.

9. Discussion Method

This method is found quite suitable for those topics in science which cannot be easily explained by demonstration or other such techniques. The discussion may be about a certain specimen or model or chart.

In this method the topics for discussion is announced to the students well in advance. The teacher gives a brief introduction about the contents of the topic and them suggests to his students various reference books, text books and other books. Students are then required to go through the relevant pages of these books and come prepared from a discussion of the topic on a specified day. During actual discussion period teachers poses a few problems and thus provides the necessary motivation. The students are then asked to answer the question one by one and when ever thinks fit advises some students not to go out of the scope of a particular question or topic under consideration. This check is essential otherwise immature students may go out of the scope of the topic.

Following points if kept in view will help make the discussion successful.

(*i*) The topics for discussion should be of common interest of students.

(*ii*) Teacher should establish a favourable atmosphere in the class before starting the discussion.

(*iii*) Teacher should see that every one participates in the discussion. The whole essence of discussion is "Thinking together".

(*iv*) The teacher should talk to the bare minimum and also should not allow any one student to dominate the whole discussion.

(*v*) It is for teacher to see that the discussion remains a discussion and it does not change into a debate.

(*vi*) Teacher should keep a check on answers of the students and should not allow a student to go beyond the scope of a topic under discussion.

(*vii*) Teacher has to maintain discipline and he should see that only one student speaks at a time.

10. Inductive – Deductive Method

It is a combination of two methods. To be able to understand this combination it is necessary to understand them separately.

I. Inductive Method

In this method one is led from concrete to abstract, particular to general and from complex to general rule. In this method we prove a universal law by showing that if it is true in a particular case it is also true in other similar cases.

This method has been found to be quite suitable for teaching of science because most of the principles of science or the conclusions are results of induction. This process of arriving at generalisation can be illustrated as under.

Illustration. Take a piece of blue litmus paper and dip it in a test tube containing hydrochloric acid, observe the change in colour. (It turns red.)

Take another piece of blue litmus paper and dip it in a test-tube containing nitric acid. Observe the change in colour. (It turns red.)

Repeat the experiments with other acids in different test tubes (e.g. oxalic acid, acetic acid etc.). (In each case blue litmus turns red.)

From the above experiments we can make a generalisation that *acid turn blue litmus red.*

Following the same procedure the students may be asked to drop a piece of chalk, duster, books, pen, pencil etc. and observe him falling these on earth. From these observations it can then be easily generalised that *all substances are attracted by earth.*

Merits of the Inductive Method

(*i*) It helps understanding.

(*ii*) It is a scientific method.

(*iii*) It develops scientific attitude.

(*iv*) It is a logical method and develops critical thinking and habit of keen observations.

(*v*) It is a psychological method and provides ample scope for students activities.

(*vi*) It is based on actual observations, thinking and experimentation.

(*vii*) It keeps alive the students interest because they move from known to unknown.

(*viii*) It curbs the tendency to learn by rote and also reduces home work

(*ix*) It develops self-confidence.

(*x*) It develops the habit of intelligent hard work.

Drawbacks of Inductive Method

This method suffers from the following limitations

(*i*) It is limited in range and cannot be used in solving and understanding all the topics in science.

(*ii*) The generalization obtained from a few observations are not the complete study of the topic. To fix the topic in the mind of the learner a lot of supplementary work and practice is needed.

(*iii*) Inductive reasoning is not absolutely conclusive. The generalization has been done from the study of a few (three or four) cases. The process thus establishes certain degree of probability which can be increased by increasing the number of valid cases

(*iv*) This method needs a lot of time and energy and thus it is time consuming and laborious method.

(*v*) This method is not found to be suitable in higher classes because some of the unnecessary details and explanations may make teaching dull and boring.

(*vi*) The use of this method should be restricted and confined to understanding the rules in the early stages.

(*vii*) This method may be considered complete and perfect only if the generalisation arrived at by induction can be verified through deductive method.

II. Deductive Method

Deductive method is opposite of inductive method. In this method the learner proceeds from general to particular, from abstract to concrete. Thus in this method facts are deduced or analysed by the application of established formula or experimentation. In this case the formula is accepted by the learner as a duly established fact.

In this method teacher announces the topics of the day and he also gives the relevant formula/rule/law/principle etc. The law/formula is also explained to the students with the help of certain examples which are solved on the black board. From these students get the idea of use or application of the concerned law/principle/formula. Then the problems are given to the students who solve the problems following the same method as explained to them earlier by the teacher. Students also memorise the results for future application.

Following example illustrates the procedure.

Principle: Cooling is caused by evaporation.

Confirmation by Application: It can be confirmed by numerous application, such as, by wearing wet clothes, observing feeling after taking bath, by applying alcohol on your hand etc.

Merits of the Deductive Method

(*i*) It is short and time saving and so this method is liked by authors and teachers.

(*ii*) It is quite a suitable method for lower classes.

(*iii*) It glorifies memory because students are required to memorise a large number of laws, formulae etc.

(*iv*) For practice and revision of topic it is an adequate and advantageous method.

(*v*) It supplements inductive method and thus completes the process of inductive – deductive method.

(*vi*) It enhances speed and efficiency in solving problems.

Limitations

(*i*) It is not a scientific method because the approach of this method is confirmatory and not explanatory.

(*ii*) It encourages rote memory because pure deductive work requires some law; principle formula for every type of problem and it demands blind memorisation of large number of such laws/formulae etc.

(*iii*) Being an unscientific method it does not impart any training in scientific method.

(*iv*) It causes unnecessary and heavy burden on the brain which may some times result in brain fag.

(*v*) In this method memory becomes more important than understanding and intelligence which is educationally not sound.

(*vi*) It is an unpsychological method because the facts and principles are not found by the students themselves.

(*vii*) In this method students cannot become active learners.

(*viii*) It is not suitable for development of thinking, reasoning and discovery.

Conclusion

A careful consideration of merits and limitations of these two methods leads in to conclude that Inductive Method is the fore- runner of Deductive Method. For effective teaching of science, both inductive and deductive approaches should be used because no one is complete without the other. Induction leaves the learner at a point where he cannot stop and the after work has to be done and completed by deduction. Deduction is a process that is particularly suitable for final statement and induction is most suitable for exploration fields. Induction gives the lead and deduction follows. In science if we want to teach about *composition of water* then its composition is determined by a endiometer tube (inductive process) and confirmed by the process of electrolysis of water (deductive process).

11. Scientific Method

This method of teaching of science is based upon the process of finding out the results by attacking a problem in a number of definite steps. It is possible to train the students in scientific method. In this method student is involved in finding out the answer to a given scientific problem and thus actually it is a type of discovery method.

Fitzpatrick defines science as, "science is a cumulative and endless series of empirical observations which result in the formation of concepts and theories, with both concepts and theories being subject to modification in the light of further empirical observation. Science is both a body of knowledge and the process of acquiring and refining knowledge".

Considering this definition of science it becomes imperative that the students be exposed to the scientific way of finding out. Scientific method of teaching helps to develop the power of reasoning, application of scientific knowledge, critical thinking and positive attitude, in the learner.

This method proceeds in the following steps:

(*i*) Problem in identified.

(*ii*) Some hypothesis are framed and these are proposed for testing.

(*iii*) Experiments are then devised to test the proposed hypothesis.

(*iv*) Data is collected from observations and the collected data is then interpreted.

(*v*) Finally conclusions are drawn to accept, reject or modify the proposed hypothesis.

Scientific method is therefore a well sequenced and structured method for finding the results through experiments.

Role of Teacher

For the success of scientific method the role of teacher is very important. He should act as a coinvestigator along with students and must also find sufficient and must also find sufficient time and have patience to attend to students' problems. Under the proper guidance of the teacher the science laboratory should become the hub for implementations of this method.

Merits

Scientific method has following advantages:

(*i*) Students learn science of their own and teacher works only as a guide.

(*ii*) It helps students to become real scientists as they learn to identify and formulate scientific problems.

(*iii*) It provides to students a training in techniques of information processing

(*iv*) It develops a habit of logical thinking in the students as they are required to interpret data and observations.

(*v*) It helps to develop intellectual honesty in students.

(*vi*) It helps the students to learn to see relationships and pattern among things and variables.

(*vii*) It provides the students a training in the methods and skills of discovering new knowledge in science.

Limitations

Some important limitations of the method are as under:

(*i*) It is a long, drawn out and time consuming method.

(*ii*) It can never become a full fledged method of learning science.

(*iii*) Due to lack of exposure to this method most of the science teachers fail to implement it successfully.

(*iv*) This method is suitable only for very bright and creative students.

12. Problem Solving Method

In this method of teaching science the students is required to solve a problem by an experimental design making use of his previous knowledge. Hence the method is almost similar to scientific method and involves almost those very steps for its implementation. Since the method is similar to scientific method so it has the same advantages and limitations as discussed for a scientific method.

3.3 CHOICE OF THE METHOD

In the previous pages a number of methods for teaching of science have been discussed. Some of them have been recommended for use, some have been disapproved and some have been recommended for use with caution. Out of the methods available a choice is not entirely left to the whims of the teacher but has to be made by the teacher in the light of facilities available and nature of work to be done. This does not mean that a teacher may select any one method and then cling to it lavishly throughout his service or even an entire academic session. This is a great mistake because each method has its own merits. Our preference for any one of the methods deprives us of the merits of other method. A good teacher should therefore try to imbibe the good qualities of all methods instead of depending on any one method. The teacher should keep himself on the right side of every method. The best method of a teacher is his own individualised and personalised method which is the result of his varied and long experience in teaching. Some of the points which a teacher should keep in mind are as under:

(*i*) Heuristic approach be used to start a lesson. Thus the lesson be introduced in a problematic way so that the students feel that they are going to learn some thing really useful and worth learning.

(*ii*) He should choose a pupil–dominated method in preference to a teacher dominated method.

(*iii*) He should have a bright manner of presentation and should illustrate his lesson with experiments, pictures, charts, diagrams etc. specimens and models are preferred for illustration

(*iv*) Teaching should be made a cooperative enterprise. Teacher should give maximum opportunity of participation to the students so that they feel that their active participation in quite important for the solution of problem and successful growth of the subject.

(*v*) Teacher should made all possible efforts to properly correlate the topic in hand with other subjects.

(*vi*) Teacher should avoid the use of difficult phrases, scientific expressions and lengthy definitions.

(*vii*) Though Heuristic approach dominates yet the historical method of teaching be utilized at places and the lives and achievements of famous scientists be told to the students. These are a source of inspiration to the students.

(*viii*) Instructional method and plans must be flexible. In a lesson if, in addition to planned illustrations and experiments students want some more experimental evidence then the teacher should make all possible efforts to satisfy the students.

(*ix*) After a constant use of some method teacher can break the monotony by using project method and laboratory method.

Thus we conclude that no single method could be the best method and a good teacher will have to evolve his own individual method consisting of good points of all the methods. He will never become a slave to any method and will remain a true master of all of them.

CHAPTER 4

Teaching Aids

4.1 INTRODUCTION

Teaching aids or audiovisual aids should be used to supplement the process of teaching. Most of the teaching aids are sensory aids and their function is to make teaching. Concrete, effective and interesting. Teaching aids can broadly be classified as under:

Those arising from:

(*i*) direct sensory contact

(*ii*) pictures, charts etc.

(*iii*) oral or printed words

First, two types are teaching aids are found to be more useful. It must always be remembered that a teaching aid should be used only to make class teaching more effective. *Even the best one of the teaching aids cannot be a substitute for class teaching.*

For a science teacher these teaching aids are all the more important as these help him to make his lesson more illustrative and explanatory.

4.2 IMPORTANCE AND NEED OF TEACHING AIDS

(*i*) These aids help the teacher in getting the attention of his students.

(*ii*) These aids help in creating the interest of the student in the topic and activate the mental process of the students.

(*iii*) The student gets an opportunity to get a first hand experience by visualising some concrete things, living specimens and actual demonstrations etc.

(*iv*) Use of teaching aids help to have a clear conception of ideas, information, facts and principles.

(*v*) It helps the students in understanding some complicated and difficult concepts.

(*vi*) They provide an opportunity for a change in the monotonous atmosphere that generally prevails in a class room.

(*vii*) They provide an opportunity for a better support between the teacher and his pupil.

(*viii*) They help the students to develop a scientific attitude.

(*ix*) They provide a training in scientific method.

(*x*) They can be used in bigger classes.

(*xi*) Use of such aids is based on the principles of psychology.

4.3 PRINCIPLES FOR USE OF TEACHING AIDS

Teaching aids should be used properly to make teaching more effective. Teaching can because more effective if such aids are used widely but the use of such aids cannot provide a guarantee of good teaching. Following points are important for a proper use of teaching aids.

(*i*) Teaching aids should be woven with class-room teaching and these aids should be used only to supplement the oral and written work being done in the class.

(*ii*) While making use of any teaching aid an effort be made that the teaching aids being used in any class are in confirmity with the intellectual level of the students and is in accordance with the previous experience of the students.

(*iii*) Only such aids the preferred which provide a stimulus to the students for greater thinking and activity.

(*iv*) If possible actual specimens be preferred to a photograph or a slide of a specimen.

(*v*) The teaching aid used should be exact, accurate and real as far as practicable.

(*vi*) The Teacher should use a teaching aid only when he is quite sure about handling a specific teaching aid. For handling some aids (e.g. operating a projector etc.) training is provided by various authorities. For this purpose more information can be obtained from local SCERT or directly from NCERT, New Delhi.

(*vii*) Teaching aids used be such as are closely related to pupils experiences.

(*viii*) The teacher should use a teaching aid only after a proper planning so that the aid is used exactly at the point; in the process of teaching, where it best fits in the process of teaching.

(*ix*) Teacher should see that a follow up programme follows the lesson wherein a teaching aid has been used.

(*x*) Teacher should carry out occasional evaluation about the use, function and effect of a teaching aid on the learning process.

4.4 TYPES OF TEACHING AIDS

For convenience of discussion the teaching aids may be grouped as under:

(*i*) Visual aids

(*ii*) Aural aids

(*iii*) Audio-visual aids

(*iv*) Activity aids and

(*v*) Memory aids

I. Visual Aids

Under this head we will take of following types of teaching aids.

(a) Display Boards such as Chalk boards or Black boards, Flannel boards, Bulletin boards, Magnetic board etc.

(b) Charts, pictures and models.

Visual aids are those which can be appreciated and understood by seeing them only.

(a) **Display Boards**

It is any flat surface that can be used to white information to be communicated. At present for this purpose the use is made of *black board* or *chalk board*, *bulletin board*, *flannel board*, *magnetic board* etc.

Though material for display on such a board can be collected from any source even from a text book but for being effective the material should be displayed in such a way that it is eye catching, colourful and purposeful.

Black Board or Chalk Board

It is one of the most common visual aids in use. It is a slightly abrasive writing surface made of wood, ply, hard board, cement, ground glass, asbestos, state, plastic etc. with black, green or bluish green paint on it. Details of various types of chalk boards and their arrangement for a science room or science laboratory have been given in the lessons dealing with these topics. A chalk board is generally installed facing the class which is either built into the wall or fixed and framed on the wall and provided with a ledge to keep the chalk sticks and duster. Portable chalk boards are also available these days. Such chalk boards can be placed on a stand with adjustable height. Generally white chalk sticks are used for writing on the black board or chalk board but some times coloured chalk sticks are also used. The coloured chalk sticks are used for better illustration.

Characteristics of a Good Chalk Board. Some of the characteristics of a good chalk board are as follows:

(*i*) Its surface should be rough enough so that it is capable of holding the writing on the board.

(*ii*) Its surface should be dull so that it can eliminate glare.

(*iii*) Its surface should be such that the writing on the board can be easily removed by making use of a cloth or a foam duster.

(*iv*) Its height should be so adjusted that it is within the easy reach of the teacher and is easily visible to the students.

Effective Use of Chalk-Board. We find that chalk board is the most common teaching aid used by the teacher for writing important points, drawing illustrations, solving problems etc. The science teacher should keep the following points in mind to use the chalk board effectively.

(*i*) Write in a clear and legible handwriting the important points on the chalk board but avoid over crowding of information on the chalk board.

(*ii*) The size of the words written on black board should be such that they can be seen even by the back-benchers. The letters should not be less than one inch in height. The recommended height of letters on a chalk board in between 6 cm to 8 cm. For this the teacher should frequently inspect his own chalk board writing from the view point of the back-bench on a corner seat.

(*iii*) There should be proper arrangement of light in the class room so that the chalk board remains glare free.

(*iv*) To emphasise some points or parts of a sketch or a diagram coloured chalks be used.

(*v*) Rub off the information already discussed in the class and noted down by the students.

(*vi*) Draw a difficult illustration before hand to save the class time.

(*vii*) Stand on one side of the chalk board while explaining some points to the students.

(*viii*) Make use of a pointer for drawing attention to the written material on the chalk board.

(*ix*) Students may be allowed to express their ideas on chalk board, or to make alterations or corrections. Some times teacher may intentionally draw some incorrect diagram and ask the students to make necessary correction, alteration etc.

(*x*) For maintenance of proper discipline in the class the teacher should always keep an eye on his class while writing on the black board.

(*xi*) For proper writing on chalk board the chalk stick be broken into two pieces and the broken end of the piece be used to start writing.

(*xii*) While writing on a chalk board keep your fingers and wrist stiff and move your arm freely.

Advantages of Chalk-board. Some of the advantages of chalk board over other visual aids are as follows:

(*i*) It is a very convenient teaching aid for group teaching.

(*ii*) It is quite economical and can be used again and again.

(*iii*) Its use is accompanied by the appropriate actions on the part of the teacher. The illustrations drawn on the black board captures students attention.

(*iv*) It is one of the most valuable supplementary teaching aid.

(*v*) It can be used as a good visual aid for drill and revision.

(*vi*) These boards can be used for drawing enlarged illustrations from the text books.

(*vii*) It is a convenient aid for giving lesson notes to the students.

Limitations of the Chalk-board. Some of the important limitations of a chalk board are as under:

(*i*) The use of chalk-board makes students very much dependent on the teacher.

(*ii*) It makes the lesson teacher paced.

(*iii*) It makes the lesson dull and of routine nature.

(*iv*) It gives no attention to the individual needs of the students.

(*v*) Due to constant use chalk boards become smooth and start glaring.

(*vi*) While using chalk-sticks to write on chalk board the teacher spreads a lot of chalk powder which is inhaled by teacher and students and it may affect their health.

(b) Bulletin Boards

It is a display board on which learning material on some scientific topic is displayed. It is generally of the size of a black-board but some times even bigger depending on the wall space available. It is generally in the form of a framed soft-board or straw-board or cork-board or rubber sheets. Such bulletin boards can be specified for individual branches of science or even for some specified science topics e.g. science puzzles, science news, science cartoons etc. such a board can also be used for displaying the best work of students. However for a all purpose bulletin board the following type of display material in recommended:

(*i*) Interesting science news.

(*ii*) Book Jackets of recently published science books.

(*iii*) Brochures.

(*iv*) Cartoons.

(*v*) Poems.

(*vi*) Sketches.

(*vii*) Pictures.

(*viii*) Photographs.

(*ix*) Thoughts.

(*x*) Announcements etc.

An effort be made to change the material on bulletin board as frequently as in practicable. Whenever the teacher starts a new topic he may ask the students to display the concerned material on the bulletin board and the teacher should specifically mention to the students the display material on the bulletin board while teaching a topic to the class. Students be asked to take the charge of bulletin board by rotation.

How to use A Bulletin Board. To make use of bulletin board as a useful teaching aid the bulletin board be used for creating interest amongst students an specific topics. For effective use of bulletin board as a teaching aid following points be kept in mind:

(*i*) Effort be made jointly by the teacher and the students to procure material from various sources on a given subject or topic.

(*ii*) Before displaying the material on the board sort out the material relevant to a specific subject or topic.

(*iii*) Make best use of your aesthetic sense to display the material on the bulletin board.

(*iv*) Do fix a title for the specific subject/topic of display material on the top centre of the bulletin board.

(*v*) It is desirable if a brief description about the specific subject or topic is fixed below the title.

(*vi*) The height of bulletin board from ground level be about 1 m.

(*vii*) The bulletin board be fixed in an area where enough lighting can be provided.

(*viii*) The material displayed should be large enough and should be provided with suitable headings.

(*ix*) Over crowding of material on bulletin board be avoided.

Advantages of Bulletin Boards. Some of the advantages of bulletin board as a teaching aid are as follows:

(*i*) It is a good supplement to class room teaching.

(*ii*) It helps in arousing the interest of students in a specific subject/topic.

(*iii*) It can be effectively used as a follow up of chalk-board.

(*iv*) Such boards add colour and liveliness and thus also have decorative value in addition to their educational value.

(*v*) Such boards can be conveniently used for introducing a topic and for its review as well.

Limitations of Bulletin Board. Some limitations in the use of bulletin boards as teaching aids are as follows:

(*i*) They cannot be used for all inclusive teaching.

(*ii*) They can be used only as supplementary aids to some other teaching aid.

(*iii*) At times it becomes very difficult to make proper selection of the display material for certain topic.

(c) Flannel Board

It is also some times referred to as *flannel graph* or *felt board.* It is made of wood, card-board or straw-board covered with coloured flannel or woolen cloth. It is one of the latest devices effectively used for science teaching. Display materials like cut-outs, pictures, drawings and light objects backed with rough surfaces like sand paper strips, flannel strips etc. will stick to flannel board temporarily.

For display purposes a flannel board of 1.5 x 1.5 m is generally used. It can be fixed next to the black-board or can be placed on a stand about one metre above the ground.

How to use a Flannel Board. Following points be kept in mind for effective use of flannel board as a teaching aid:

(*i*) The teacher should collect a large number of pictures or wall cut diagrams etc. and back them with sand paper pieces. He may then make use of these by displaying these on the board one by one, after proper selection.

(*ii*) Display the material on the flannel board in a sequence to develop the lesson.

(*iii*) Make proper use of flannel board for creating proper scenes and designs relevant to the lesson.

(*iv*) Change the display material on the board as frequently as required.

(*v*) Flannel board can be used quite effectively for showing relationship between different parts or steps of a process.

Advantages of Flannel-Board. Some of the advantages of using flannel-board as a teaching aid are as follows:

(*i*) It is quite economical and easy to handle and operate.

(*ii*) The pictures or cuttings can be easily fixed and removed when required, without spoiling the material. Thus same material can be used for display many a times.

(*iii*) Any display material on the board holds the interest of students and arrests their attention.

(*iv*) Such boards enable a teacher to talk along with changing illustrations to develop a lesson.

(d) Magnetic Chalk Board

It is a framed iron sheet having porcelain coating in black or green colour. Such a board can be used either to write with chalk sticks, glass marking pencils and crayons or to display pictures, cut-outs and light objects with disc magnets or magnetic holders.

Thus such a board functions both as a chalk board and as a flannel board. We can display visual learning material on such a board while writing key points on it. Such a board provides the flexibility of movement of visual material. It is possible to display even a three dimensional object on such a board using magnetic holders.

Since the magnetic chalk-board functions both as a chalk board and as a flannel board so various points discussed for the effective use of these boards be kept in mind while using magnetic chalk board as an effective teaching aid.

Advantages of Magnetic Chalk Board. Some of the advantages of magnetic chalk board are as follows:

(*i*) It is a versatile teaching aid that combines the advantages of both a chalk board and a flannel board.

(*ii*) It is possible to move visual material by sliding it along the surface of the board such a movement is not possible on a flannel board.

(*iii*) It is very light and can be easily taken from one place to another.

(*iv*) Such a board can be easily got prepared in the school from an iron sheet and painting with some good paint.

Charts, Pictures and Models

Charts, pictures and models also are an important teaching aids.

Charts. Sometimes charts are needed by the teacher to supplement his actual teaching. There are certain charts where in the interior of some thing is depicted e.g. various systems of human body, internal combustion engine, motor car etc.

Following points be kept in view while using charts as teaching aids:

(*i*) An effort be made to use charts prepared by students under the guidance of the teacher, however some charts may be purchased.

(*ii*) Only such charts be purchased which have bold lines and in which such colours are used as could be seen and distinguished even by the back-benchers.

(*iii*) Charts should give only the essential details.

(*iv*) Charts should be properly and clearly labelled in block letters.

Sources for Procurement of Charts

(*i*) Charts can be prepared by students and teacher.

(*ii*) Charts can be purchased.

(*iii*) Charts can be procured on a very nominal cost from the following sources:

(a) Ministry of Education, Govt. of India, Delhi.

(b) NCERT, New Delhi.

(c) Director, Extension Service of College of Education in the State.

(d) SCERT of the state.

(e) District Public Relation Officer.

Advantages of Charts

(*i*) They can be made quickly.

(*ii*) They have a better appeal.

(*iii*) Only bare essentials can be shown in the chart and unnecessary details can be avoided.

(*iv*) Charts are available from various sources.

Pictures. Pictures of gas-works, steamships, and locomotives and portraits of great men of science – physicists, chemists, biologists and astronomers – will be of great help in teaching of science provided a reference in made to them. Portraits of great scientists if displayed in science room give it the proper scientific atmosphere. These pictures, portraits etc. can be used as teaching aids and they are quite useful in a demonstration lesson. Everything a child learns can be presented graphically with the aid of pictures and brightly coloured diagrams which will excite his interest.

Following points be given due consideration while using pictures as teaching aids:

(*i*) Pictures should be bold, direct and sufficiently large.

(*ii*) Pictures should not be over loaded with information rather they should stick to the maxim, *'one picture, one idea'*.

Models. In teaching of science models are very frequently used. Various costly models are available and some of these may be available and in school laboratory. However the cost of such models should not be any hindrance to the use of models as teaching aid because a science teacher can prepare almost all types of models by making use of ingenuity. It is also possible to take some very costly models on loan or such models can even be hired. Models are very helpful in making the subject clear to the students and they also give the student an idea of the actual shape/size etc. of the article under discussion.

In using charts, pictures and models as teaching aids the teacher should be careful to plan their proper display. These should be displayed in such a way and at such a height that each student can have a detailed view of it.

Following is the list of some firms from whom scientific charts and models can be procured:

1. M/s Scientific Instruments Stores, J-355, New Rajinder Nagar, New Delhi.
2. M/s Educational Aids and Charts, 20, I Block, Kumara Park, West Extension, Bangalore-20.
3. M/s Variety Teaching Aids, Bagalkot, Distt. Bijapur.
4. M/s Educational Emporium, 15-A, Chittranjan Avenue, Calcutta-7.
5. M/s Oxford University Press, Appollo Bunder, Bombay.
6. M/s School Aids Manufacturing Co., 12-Gun Boat Street, Fort, Bombay-1.
7. The Director, Survey of India, Hathi Barkala Road, Dehradun (UP).
8. M/s Hobby Centre, Mount Road, Madras-2.

II. Aural Aids

In this type the following aids are considered:

(*i*) Broadcast talks,
(*ii*) Gramophone lectures, and
(*iii*) Tape recordings.

Broadcast Talks. All India Radio has in its regular feature some programmes meant for school children. In such a programme generally talks on educational matters or on scientific topics are broadcasted. Such a talk in quite useful for students as also for science teacher. The topic, date and time of broadcast of such talks are given in advance by All India Radio. A school can take benefit of such talks only if it possesses a good radio set and a period is provided in the school time-table for listening such talks. Such an arrangement can be worked out by the school authorities and then teacher can refer to such talks while teaching his class. It is also possible to synchronise the broad cast talk on some topic with the actual teaching of that topic in a class.

Some handicaps of such broadcast task are listed here.

(*i*) Sometimes when the receiving set is not working satisfactorily there prevails a sense of strain in the class room.

(*ii*) Some students are poor listeners and may not be benefited by such talks although they benefit by normal teaching through questions, demonstrations and reading.

For the maximum utility of such talks following points be kept in view:

(*i*) The students with bad hearing be seated on front seats.

(*ii*) To keep students interest alive in such talks teacher should tell his students in advance a few questions which they have to answer after the talk.

(*iii*) Only short duration talks be arranged.

Such talks cannot be a substitute to the actual teaching and such a talk is only to help in teaching.

Gramophone Lectures and Tape Recordings. Another teaching aid available to a science teacher is records of short talks an interesting scientific topics by eminent scientists, doctors etc. Magnetic tapes of such recorded talks are now available and the talk can be easily reproduced in the class room. These talks provide an inspiration to the students and such a talk once recorded can be used again and again. Such recording can either be used to introduce a topic or to develop a topic. Even the voice of different birds and animals can be recorded and reproduced in the class while teaching about such animals or birds.

III. Audio-Visual Aids

In this catagory those teaching aids are included which involve the use of two of our senses *i.e.* hearing and seeing. These are classified as (*i*) optical aids and (*ii*) Television.

Optical Aids

Some such aids are discussed here. *Magic Lantern (or Glass slide projector).*

Psychologists have now confirmed that a child grasps abstract facts slowly and can only remember a name which recalls some definite reality. Thus he should be confronted with visual teaching aids to broaden his experience.

A *magic lantern* is a simple device used to project pictures from a glass slide on a screen or wall. Teacher can make use of this device when he intends to show some small figure or illustration to whole class. Many a schools have a *magic lantern* in their laboratories as it is not very costly slides are readily available in the market on various science topics. These can also be got prepared on demand and the cost of such a slide is quite reasonable. Such slides can even be prepared by science teacher himself after some practical training which can be provided by extension service department of training colleges.

Epidiascope

Epidiascope is a more costly instrument but it can project opaque objects as well as transparent objects. The pictures projected by epidiascope are much brighten and needs a less powerful light so that room need not be absolutely dark. Epidiascope can be used to project any picture, map, diagram, photograph or small object. No slide is needed for projection with an epidiascope.

The name *epidiascope* is given to this machine because of the fact that it works, as an *episcope* when it is used to throw the image of an opaque object. This machine can be used to project slides and this is possible just by moving a lower provided for the purpose. When it is used to project a slide then at serves as a *diascope*. Thus *epidiascope* is a combination of these two *i.e. episcope* and *diascope*.

Advantages of Epidiascope. In comparison to other projection machines *epidiascope* has some advantages. Some of these are as follows:

(*i*) It can be operated in a room which may not be absolutely dark.

(*ii*) With the help of this machine original colours of the picture or photograph can be projected.

(*iii*) The projection on the screen can be kept for some time during which teacher can explain and discuss it in the class.

(*iv*) It provides teacher an option to handle the lesson according to himself.

Following points provide useful hints for the proper handling of an epidiascope.

(*i*) The apparatus works well in a dark room.

(*ii*) While projecting with an epidiascope an effort be made to keep exposed to the head of the lamp for minimum time delicate pictures, photographs or other such objects.

(*iii*) The person handling the apparatus must be given some practical training before he is allowed to handle the machine.

Film Projector, Micro-Projector, Film-Strip Projector

There are further improvements on the teaching aids discussed so far. These have brought about a revolution in teaching of science. Science films are shown to the students to illustrate various applications and uses of science as also to supplement the class room teaching. Both type of films have some basic objectives to serve.

Film Strip-Projector

It is an improvement on magic lantern and this machine can be used to project many a topics on a single strip. One such strip generally consists of 40-100 separate pictures and such film strips are available on loan from Central Film Library, NCERT, New Delhi. On such a film strip pictures concerning one topic are arranged in a definite order.

This machine can be easily handled by the science teacher. The machine is operated by hand and thus can be stopped at the discretion of the teacher whenever he wants to explain some aspect of a topic being shown on machine.

Micro-Projector

This is most commonly used in biology teaching for showing microscopic slides, small living specimen and growth or crystals. This projector is generally operated in a dark room. The projection can be taken on vertical screen if whole class is expected to see it. However such a film cannot be distinctly seen by a student if he is sitting at a distance more than 12 feet from the screen.

Film Projector

This machine is used for showing science films. Some good science films on various topics are available and these can be had on loan some times even free of charge from the source, given below:

(*i*) Central Film Library, NCERT, New Delhi.

(*ii*) U.S. Information Service, New Delhi.

(*iii*) British High Commissions Office, New Delhi.

(*iv*) Some Other Embassies, New Delhi.

For projecting this films in school generally 16 mm projector ('RCA', 'Bell and Havell') are used. These 16 mm projectors are less costly and easier to transport as compared to a 35 mm projector.

Advantages of Motion Pictures. There are some definite advantages of motion pictures to be used as teaching aids, some of these are as follows:

(*i*) They draw attention of the students.

(*ii*) They help to bring past to the class-room.

(*iii*) It is possible to reduce or enlarge the size of the object by using the machine.

(*iv*) They can be used to show a process which a naked human eye cannot see without its aid.

(*v*) They can be used to show a record of an event.

(*vi*) They can serve a large class at a time.

(*vii*) They provide a good aesthetic experience.

(*viii*) They help in understanding relationship between things, ideas and events.

Precautions. The teacher should take the following precautions whenever he wants to use a film projection as a teaching aid:

(*i*) He should satisfy himself about the lighting management and seating arrangement in the room where such a film show is to be given.

(*ii*) He should himself see the film before hand.

(*iii*) He should give a complete background of the film to the students before the actual screening of the film.

(*iv*) He should see that complete calm and peace is maintained during the screening of the film.

(*v*) Immediately after the film show, he should invite comments, questions etc. from the students and try to answer all the quarries of the students.

(*vi*) He should encourage some of his students to write articles etc. based on the film show and such articles etc., may be shown on well magazine, may be printed in school magazine.

Television

The role of television in the present day world is becoming more and more important and it is one of the most important teaching aids. It combines the advantages of a radio (broad cast) and of a film. This can be used for mass education and now U.G.C. programmes are a regular feature on "Door Darshan". The topics of discussion are announced in advance and lesson from well qualified persons and specialists in their fields are shown on TV. Teacher can easily plan his work accordingly and in this way he can make use of TV as a teaching aid.

IV. Activity Aids

Activity aids include

(*i*) Science museum.

(*ii*) Nature study garden.

(*iii*) Science fairs

(*i*) Science Museum

A museum ought to be a very valuable part of a science department in school. Nature study and chemistry provide many examples of things which may be kept in such a museum. Though the ideal way to gain knowledge is to observe objects and phenomenon in their natural setting but in the present educational set up there is only a little opportunity for this. A science museum helps in this aspect. Museum not only provides necessary help in teaching but also helps in creating the right type of scientific atmosphere in the school.

A good museum should be scholar built. An effort be made to avoid exhibiting ready made articles. Change is the law of nature and it is always good to replace with better objects those exhibits which have become unsatisfactory either because of their age of because of their use. The teacher should make all efforts to enrich the science museum and should encourage his students to make new additions to the school museum. The museum should consist of:

(*i*) Dry exhibits such as leaves, roots, weeds, specimen of ores and minerals etc.

(*ii*) Fish, snakes, water-weeds, etc.

(*iii*) Butterflies, insects and shell-fish are exhibited in boxes having cork bottom. Silver plated pins should be used for fixing these objects to avoid rusting. It is always advisable to place some naphthalene balls in the boxes to avoid danger from moths.

In addition to these a science museum may exhibit models of various mechanical devices, specimens of some local industrial products, various stages in the manufacture of items such as a match box, pencil etc. can also be depicted. Some of the preparations done by the students can also be depicted in the science museum.

Some other important points about a science museum are:

(*i*) Systematic arrangement of various exhibits, and

(*ii*) Clear and complete description of various parts of the exhibits.

For this purpose an ideal arrangement will be that a card of suitable size (5" x 4") be attached to each item exhibited in the museum and the following information be typed on this card or written in a good hand writing on the card.

(*i*) Scientific as also the common name of the exhibit. For biological specimen the family to which the exhibit belongs should also be indicated.

(*ii*) The place where from the exhibit has been obtained and the other relevant information.

(*iii*) Importance of the exhibit.

The language used for providing the above information should be simple and all efforts be made to avoid phrases and technical terms in the description of the exhibit.

Care for Living Things. Provisions must be made for caring for all types of living things in the museum. A variety of suitable containers be made available for housing them. The wise teacher will always have the following containers available insect cages, small animal cages, aquariums, and terrariums.

Insects

For housing we can use small cake pans, coffee cans, or covers from ice cream cartons for cover and base. Roll wire screening into cylinder to fit base and lace together with strand of wire.

Cut windows in paper coffee container, oatmeal box, or shoe box. Glue Saran, cellophane, silk, or nylon stocking over windows.

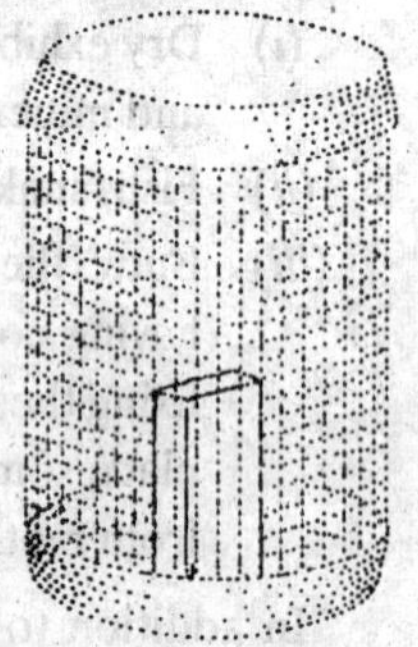

Fig. 4.1

Fill wide-mouthed quart or gallon pickle jar with soil to within two inches of top of jar. Cover jar with nylon stocking and place jar in pan of water. Can be used for ants, termites, worms, etc. Cover jar with black construction paper after putting in insects.

Animals (Fig. 4.3)

Some of the insect containers described above can also be used for small animals. For housing larger animals we can easily construct cages.

A cage for a larger animal can be made from wire screening. Cut the wire screening as shown. Fold where dotted lines are shown. Tack or staple three sides to a wooden base. Hook one side to enable easy cleaning.

Terrarium. Get six pieces of glass any size and place them as follows: arrange glass according to diagram (Fig. 4.4). Use tape one inch wide (plastic or adhesive) on joints and rub very hard to make

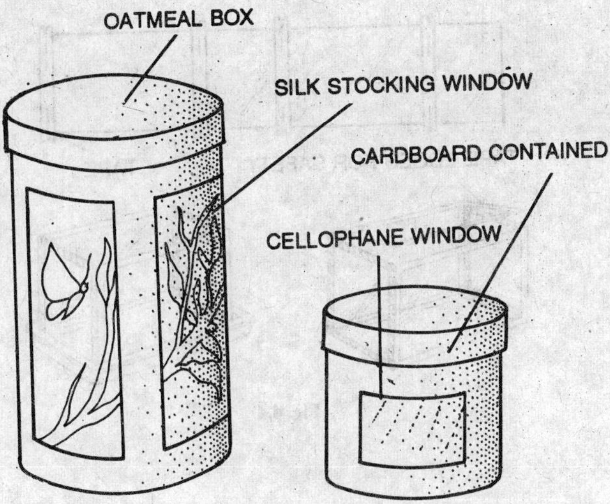

Fig. 4.2

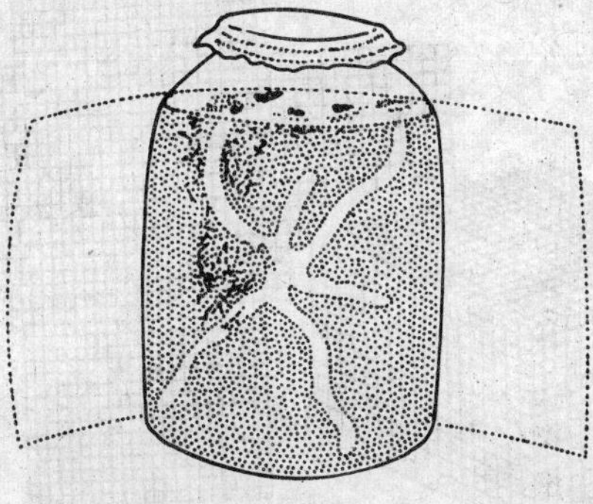

Fig. 4.3

sure of good adhesion. Turn over and put tape on other side in same manner. Place tape on lid according to diagram and another piece for a handle. Place glass terrarium in cookie or cake pan.

Some suggestions for housing some of the more commonly used animals are given below.

Housing. Wooden box or crate of about 24 in. x 16 in. x 12 in. with door.

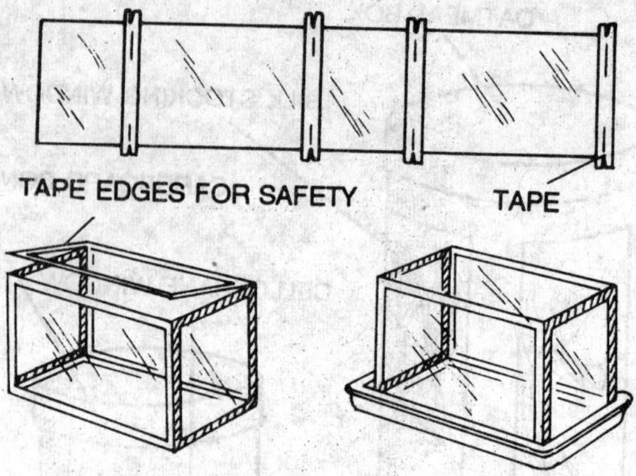

Fig. 4.4

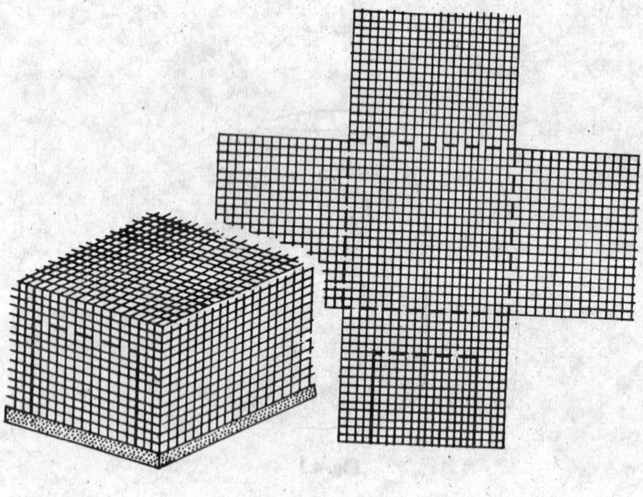

Fig. 4.5

Metal or wire mesh (gnaw through wood); removable solid bottom for cleaning; woodshavings, sawdust, or strips of paper on floor of cage, bottle with one hole stopper and tube for water.

Wire screen home; woodshavings, sawdust, strips of newspaper; water bottle mentioned previously.

Should be wire mesh as rabbits need a great deal of ventilation; use type of wire cage as shown but enlarge to at least 3 ft. x 2 ft. x 2 ft; floor should be perforated.

Depends on variety; some need aquarium; some woodland terrarium; some combination of two; escape easily so place tight cover on them.

Wire mesh; wooden branch for support; must be solid with tight cover as snakes escape easily.

(ii) Nature Study Garden

Nature study garden is a must for every school involved in nature study. Such a garden should have a pond as well. Teacher should encourage his students to maintain the nature study garden of the school and to maintain as many varieties, of plants and animals in this garden, as is possible. These plants and animals can then be shown to the students while actually discussing about them in the class.

(iii) Science Fairs and Exhibitions in Schools

We find that functions such as prize distribution, parents day, sports day etc. form a regular feature of most schools. Just like these

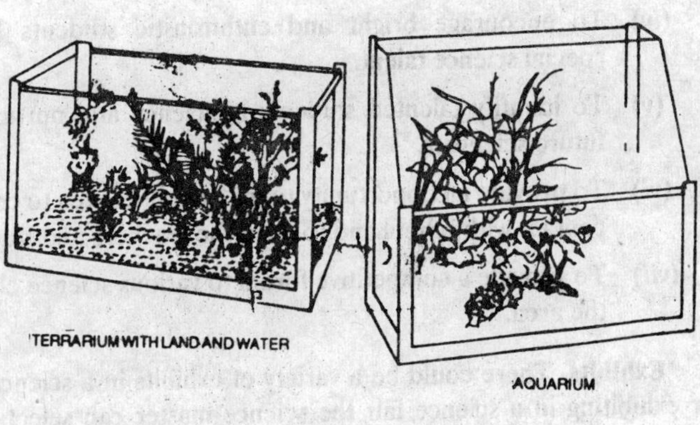

Fig. 4.6

functions an effort should be made to hold an annual science fair or exhibition may be along with any of these days. A science fair provides an excellent opportunity for display and dissemination of various activities that are being carried over by the science club. A science fair can also serve the purpose of acquainting the parents in particular and people of locality in general with the diverse nature of scientific work that is undertaken in the school. The organisation of a science fair or a science exhibition can easily be entrusted to the school science club. In recent years various government agencies encourage the organisation of science fairs and science exhibitions. The encouragement is provided in the form of financial and other help. Such fairs are encouraged by NCERT and SCERT of various states.

NCERT (National Council of Educational Research and Training) has outlined the following objectives for organising science fairs.

(*i*) To give impetus and provide encouragement to students to try out their ideas and to apply their knowledge of science into some creative channel.

(*ii*) To provide opportunities to students to see for themselves some achievements of their colleagues and in this way stimulate them to plan their occur projects.

(*iii*) To make science activities more popular amongst the students thereby hoping to improve standards of performance.

(*iv*) To encourage bright and enthusiastic students having special science talent.

(*v*) To identify talented students in science and nurture the future scientists.

(*vi*) To provide an opportunity to the people of area to come in contact with school and to meet the teachers and students.

(*vii*) To provide a competitive forum to various science clubs in the area.

Exhibits. There could be a variety of exhibits in a science fair. For exhibiting in a science fair the science master can select a few interesting experiments, charts, working models of useful appliances specimen collected by students during excursions, applications of scientific principles to daily life, scientific toys etc. For sake of convenience exhibits can be classified as under:

(*i*) Experiments

(*ii*) Models

(*iii*) Specimens

(*iv*) Collections

(*v*) Improvised apparatus

(*vi*) Charts and diagrams

(*vii*) Investigatory projects.

Organisation of a Science Fair. Whenever a science teacher plans to organise a science fair he should inform his students about it well in advance. Then he should start to find a good and suitable location in the school where such fair can be organised. Having located a suitable place he should start planning or arrangements of exhibits. In this planning he should always keep in mind that time consuming exhibits are spread all over the available space and are not accumulated at one place.

He should then train some selected students to act as students guide. Science teacher should see that these students volunteers can guide the visitors and can explain to them various scientific principles involved in any exhibit.

Evaluation. To encourage the participants some prizes in the form of general science books or merit certificates may be instituted and awarded to pupils whose exhibits have been adjudged best by a panel of judges. For purpose of award of prizes various exhibits at a science fair be classified in various catagories and prizes be awarded separately for some good entries in each class. While judging an exhibit some criteria on the following lines may be used by the judges. Various aspects be given the following weightage.

1. Scientific approach 30%
2. Originality 20%

3. **Technical skill** **20%**
4. **Thoroughness** **10%**
5. **Dramatic value** **10%**
6. **Personal Interview** **10%**

CHAPTER 5

Planning Science Lessons

5.1 INTRODUCTION

Though a syllabus is prescribed for each class yet the teacher is at liberty to draw up his own teaching syllabus. It is best to organise the teaching syllabus around a few broad areas of experience of pupils. For this purpose the syllabus is divided into a number of units.

5.2 UNIT PLANNING

A *unit* is a related learning segment made up of a few lessons along with an outline of its actual execution in the class room. Thus a unit will consist of both the subject matter and methodology of its delivery to students.

Hoover defines unit as, "The teaching unit is a group of related concepts from which a given set of instructional and educational experiences is desired. Unit normally range for three to six weeks long".

In view of Preston, a unit is a large chunk or a block of related subject matter as can be over viewed by the learner.

After having divided the prescribed syllabus into a number of teaching units the teachers will decide the time that could be allotted to each unit. After that he can break up each unit in a number of lessons and each lesson should be complete in itself. After this the teacher will enter in his diary the scheme of work under the headings. (See Table P. 118).

Some of the advantages of unit planning are as under:

(*i*) It provides a basic course structure around which specific class activities can be organised.

(*ii*) It enables the teacher to integrate the basic course concepts and those of related areas into various teaching experiences.

(*iii*) It provides an opportunity to the teacher to keep a balance between various dimensions of the prescribed course.

Unit No....................

Date	*Course content*	*Demonstration*	*Equipment material*	*Student's activities*	*Remarks/ References*

(*iv*) It enables the teacher to break away from traditional text-book teaching.

If the prescribed course has to be course has to be covered in a number of years then it is unwise to distribute the course in units spread over a number of years.

5.3 LESSON PLANNING

A proper planning of the lessons is key to effective teaching. The teacher must know in advance the subject matter and mode of its delivery in the class room. This gives the teacher an idea of how to develop the key concepts and how to correlate them to real life situations and how to conclude the lesson. Lesson planning is also essential because effective learning takes place only if the subject matter is presented in an integrated and correlated manner and is related to the pupil's environment. Though lesson planning requires a hard work but it is rewarding too. L.B. Stands conceives a lesson as 'plan of action' implemented by the teacher in the classroom. According to G.H. Green, "The teacher who has planned his lesson wisely related to his topic and to his class room without any anxiety, ready to embark with confidence upon a job he understands and prepared to carry it to a workmanable conclusion. He has foreseen the difficulties that are likely to arise, and prepared himself to deal with them. He knows the aims that his lesson is intended to fulfill, and he has marshalled his own resources for the purpose. And because he is free of anxiety, he will be able coolly to estimate the value of his work as the lesson proceeds, equally aware of failure and success and prepared to learn from both".

5.4 ADVANTAGES OF LESSON PLANNING

Some of the advantages of planning a lesson are as under:

(*i*) Lesson planning makes the work regular, organised and more systematic.

(*ii*) It induces confidence in the teacher.

(*iii*) It makes teacher quite conscious of the aim which makes him conscious of attitudes he wants to develop in his students.

(*iv*) It saves a lot of time.

(*v*) It helps in making correlation between the concepts with the pupils environment.

(*vi*) It stimulates the teacher to ask striking questions.

(*vii*) It provides more freedom in teaching.

5.5 FEATURES OF A LESSON PLAN

Some Important features of a good lesson plan are as under:

(*i*) *Objectives:* All the congnitive objectives that are intended to be fulfilled should be listed in the lesson plan.

(*ii*) *Content:* The subject matter that is intended to be covered should be limited to prescribed time. The matter must be interesting and it should be related to pupil's previous knowledge. It should also be related to daily life situations.

(*iii*) *Method(s):* The most appropriate method be chosen by the teacher. The method chosen should be suitable to the subject matter to be taught. Suitable teaching aids must also be identified by the teacher. Teacher may also use supplementary aids to make his lesson more effective.

(*iv*) *Evaluation:* Teacher must evaluate his lesson to find the extent to which he has achieved the aim of his lesson. Evaluation can be done even by recapitulation of subject matter through suitable questions.

5.6 STEPS IN LESSON PLANNING -(HERBARTIAN STEPS)

Formal steps in lesson planning are:

(*i*) Introduction (or preparation)
(*ii*) Presentation
(*iii*) Association (or comparison)
(*iv*) Generalisation
(*v*) Application
(*vi*) Recaptulation

1. Introduction

It pertains to preparing and motivating children to the lesson content by linking it to the previous knowledge of the student, by arousing curiosity of the children and by making an appeal to their senses. This prepares the child's mind to receive new knowledge. This step though so important must be brief. It may involve testing of previous knowledge of the child. Some times the curiosity of pupil can be aroused by some experiment, chart, model, story or even by some useful discussion.

2. Presentation

It involves the stating of the object of lesson and exposure of students to new information. The actual lesson begins and both teacher and students participate. Teacher should make use of different teaching aids to make his lesson effective. Teacher should draw as much as is possible from the students making use of judicious questions. In science lesson it is desirable that a heuristic atmosphere prevails in the class.

3. Association

It is always desirable that new ideas or knowledge be associated to the daily life situations by citing suitable examples and by drawing comparisons with the related concepts. This step is all the more important when we are establishing principles or generalising definitions.

4. Generalisation

In science lessons generally the learning material leads to certain generalisations leading to establishment of certain formulaes, principles or laws. An effort be made that the students draw the conclusions themselves. Teacher should guide the students only if their generalisation is either incomplete or irrelevant.

5. Application

In this step of lesson plan the knowledge gained is applied to certain situations. This step is in confirmity with the general desire of the students to make use of generalisation in order to see for themselves if the generalisations are valid in certain situations or not? No lesson of science may be considered complete if such rules, principles, formula etc. are not applied to life situations.

6. Recaptulation

In this last step of his lesson plan the teacher tries to ascertain whether his students have understood and grasped the subject matter or not. This is used for assessing the effectiveness of the lesson by asking students questions on the contents of the lesson. Recaptulation can also be done by giving a short objective type test to the class or even by asking the students to label some unlabelled sketch.

One most important point to remember is that the six steps given above for lesson planning are formal Herbartian steps and teacher should not try to follow these very rigidly. These are only guide lines and in many a lessons it is not possible to follow all these steps.

There is another way of lesson planning which is gaining currency these days. It is known as *Glover Plan*. This plan has four steps as follows:

1. *Questioning.* Teacher must introduce and develop his lesson through related and sequential questions. Start the lesson by asking questions about previous knowledge of the students. The questions should then lead to new knowledge under consideration.

Lesson can also be introduced with the help of some teaching aid like a picture, chart or model etc. the introduction can also to made by describing a situation or by telling a short story.

However teacher should hear in mind that the introduction is brief and interesting.

2. *Discussion.* For discussion the class be divided into smaller groups and in such groups students be encouraged to express their

ideas and opinions freely. This helps the students in removal of their difficulties.

3. *Investigation.* The students are encouraged to do a project or investigation on the lesson topic either individually or in small groups by processing information or by laboratory work.

4. *Expression.* It concerns the strategy in which the student's and teacher's communication of ideas through observation and listening (passive expression) or through doing (active expression) or through fine and performing arts (artistic expression) or by arranging learning situations (organisational expression).

In developing a lesson a teachers must keep in mind the following psychological principles.

(*i*) *Principle of Selection and Division.* The teacher should wisely select and divide the learning material into smaller segments. It is also for the teacher to decide about the quantum of subject matter to be covered by him and that which has to be illicited from the students.

(*ii*) *Principle of Successive Clarity.* It is for the teacher to see that the different learning segments of lesson are well structured, sequenced and connected. Teacher must ensure, at each segment, that students have grasped the subject matter given to them.

(*iii*) *Principle of Integration.* Teacher should conclude his lesson only after combining various learning segments to produce some generalisation.

Design for Writing a Lesson Plan

Lecture-Cum-Demonstration Method

The style given below is generally followed for writing a lesson plan.

Class:	Date:
Subject:	Duration
Topic:	of period:

Instructional Material ______________________________

____

General Objectives ______________________________

____

Specific objectives ______________________________

____

Previous Knowledge ______________________________

____

Questions

1. ______________________________ ?
2. ______________________________ ?
3. ______________________________ ?

Introduction

Questions

1. ______________________________ ?
2. ______________________________ ?

Announcement of Aim ______________________________

____

Presentation

Matter	*Method*	*B. B. Summary*

Generalisations ______________________________

____

Applications ______________________________

____

Recaptulation

Questions

1. ______________________________?
2. ______________________________?
3. ______________________________?

House Task ______________________________

____

5.7 SPECIMEN LESSON PLAN

Class: X — Date:

Subject: Biology — Duration
Topic: Structure of human heart — of period: 40 minutes

Instructional Material (Teaching Aids)

1. Black board, duster, coloured chalks.
2. A model of human heart
3. A few actual specimens of heart some of which are dissected and at least two are in original state, dissection material such as dish, slide, pin, spirit, scissors, forceps, needle, cotton etc.

General Objectives

1. To develop scientific attitude amongst the pupil.
2. To develop power of observation and sense of enquiry amongst the pupil.
3. To develop reflective thinking in pupils.

Specific Objectives

To make students understand the structure and functioning of human heart.

Previous Knowledge

It is presumed that the students know about the various internal organs of human body.

Introduction

For introducing the lesson teacher will prick the pin in the finger of one of the students (while doing so the teacher will not say any thing and he would also see that the pin he uses for pricking should be first dipped in spirit). When the pin is pricked some blood on a slide and then he will put the following questions:

1. Can you tell me from where has this blood come?
2. Can you tell me the position of heart in human body?
3. Can you tell me some thing about the structure of human heart?

Announcement of Aim

When no satisfactory answer is given by students to question 3 above, the teacher will announce the topic by saying that, "Today we will learn about the structure and working of human heart".

Presentation

To present the lesson teacher will use the actual specimen and model of human heart. He will also instruct the students to note him what they are told and what they observe.

Matter	*Method*	*B. B. Summary*
1. The heart is situated on the left side of body below the bones of chest.	Question will be asked from students. 1. Do you observe any throbbing on the left side of your body below the chest? 2. What is it due to?	Heart
2. It is like a closed first or the shape of a *pan* leaf.		
3. It is covered from outside by their membrane called *pericardium*.	Pericardium will be shown by the teacher from actual specimen of human heart.	*Pericardium*
4. *Pericardium* protects the heart from any external shock.		

	Matter	*Method`*	*B. B. Summary*
5.	Heart is divided into two by thick muscular partition. (*i*) right side (*ii*) left side. These two halves don't communicate with each other.	Teacher will show these parts by removing wall of heart in the model. Then he will ask, how many chambers do you see?	
6.	The anterior chambers are two *auricles* and posterior are two *ventricles*.		*Auricle* *Ventricle*
7.	The auricles are communicated by ventricles through aperture called *valves*.	What is a valve?	
8.	Valve acts as a watchman because it helps to check the entry of blood from ventricles back to auricles.	What is the functions of a valve?	
9.	In the right auricle we find two large *vena cavae.* One of these bring blood from anterior portion of body (superior vena cavae) and the other from lower portion (inferior vena cavae)	How many tubes enter the right auricle?	(1) Superior vena cavae (2) Inferior vena cavae
10.	From right ventricle a pulmonary artery takes away impure blood towards the lungs for purification.	Pulmonary artery will be shown by the teacher from actual specimen.	Pulmonary artery.
11.	Pure blood from left ventricle (by pulmonary vein in left auricle) through *dorsal aorta* goes to the various parts of the body.	Dorsal Aorta will be shown to the students from the actual model of heart.	Dorsal Aorta.
12.	*Working* The impure blood from various parts of human body first of all comes in right auricles through veins. The blood goes to right ventricle by	What do you see in between the auricle and ventricle? How does the blood goes from the auricle to the ventricle? How is blood supplied	

contraction of auricles. On getting blood ventricles relaxes and simultaneously it contracts and blood is pumped. The pure blood from lungs comes in the left auricle through pulmonary veins. The auricle starts contraction and blood is forced into the ventricle through valve. At this stage the ventricle starts contraction which forces the blood into dorsal aorta and through it to different parts of human body. Thus we find that functioning of heart involves alternate contraction and relaxation.

.parts of our body? What do you understand by alternate contraction and relaxation?

Black Board Summary

A labelled diagram of human heart will be drawn on the black board. In this students will be actively involved. The diagram will show all the parts of human heart and it will not include any other part of our body.

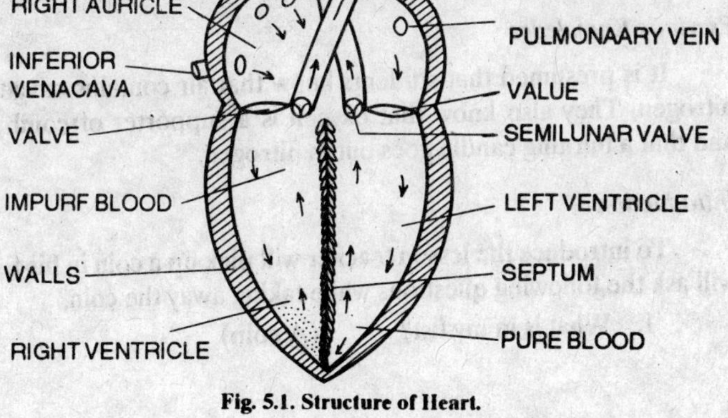

Fig. 5.1. Structure of Heart.

Recaptulation

For recaptulation students will be asked to draw a well labelled diagram of the human heart.

Home Task

Students will be asked to make a model of human heart.

SPECIMEN LESSON PLAN

Class – X
Subject – Chemistry
Topic – Composition of Air

Date –
Duration of period – 40 minutes

Instructional Materials

1. Chalk board, duster, coloured chalks.
2. Trough, jar, match box, phosphorus etc.
3. Candle, glass tumbler, house hold plate, baby feeder etc.

General Objectives

1. To develop scientific attitude amongst the pupil.
2. To develop lower of observation and sense of enquiry amongst the pupil
3. To develop reflective thinking in the pupils.

Specific Objective

To tell the students that air contains one part of oxygen and four parts of nitrogen by volume.

Previous Knowledge

It is presumed that students know that air contains oxygen and nitrogen. They also know that oxygen is a supporter of combustion and that a burning candle goes out in nitrogen.

Introduction

To introduce the lesson teacher will pick up a coin in his fist and will ask the following questions while taking away the coin,

1. What is in my fist? (A coin)

2. When the coin has been taken away,
   What is now in my hand? (Air)
3. It is possible for us to live without air? (No)
4. Name the gases present in Air? (Oxygen, Nitrogen and some CO_2, inert gases etc.).
5. What is the proportion of oxygen and nitrogen in the air?

Announcement of Air

Our not receiving a proper reply to question 5 teacher will announce the aim "Today we will try to know about the proportion of oxygen and nitrogen in air".

Generalisation

From the above experiments we conclude that oxygen and nitrogen are present, in the ratio of 1 : 4 by volume, in air.

Recapitulation

Teacher will ask the following questions for recapitulation.

(*i*) Does phosphorus burn if exposed to air?

(*ii*) What is the ratio of oxygen and nitrogen (by volume) in air?

(*iii*) Which compound is formed when phosphorus burns in air?

Home Task

Students will be asked to perform a similar experiment using a candle instead of phosphorus.

Presentation

	Matter	*Method*	*Blackboard Summary*
1.	Yellow phosphorus in air at 307K	Showing phosphorus, teacher asks, what is this? Does phosphorus burn in air?	Yellow Phosphorus It is kept under water. It burns in air.
2.	Yellow phosphorus is kept in water.	What is yellow phosphorus stored under water?	
3.	Yellow phosphorus burns in air.	What happens if a piece of yellow phosphorus is kept in air?	
4.	Fitting up the apparatus for the experiment as shown in fig. 5.	What is this? What is this? What is this? What is this?	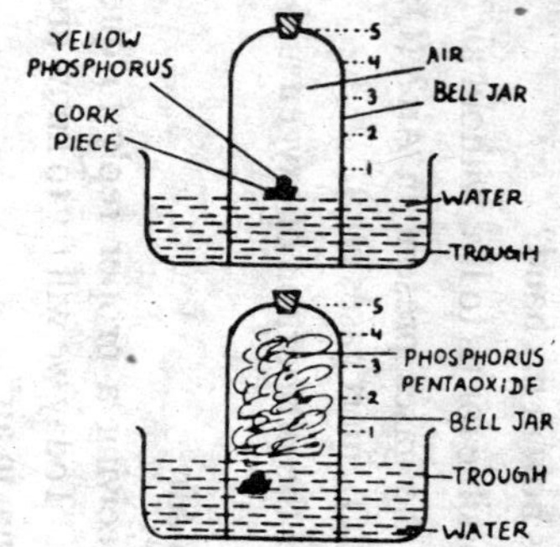
5.	Phosphorus piece is allowed to burn by touching it with hot iron rod.	What happens? Why does phosphorus burn? What is this cloud like substance?	
6.	Water rises upto mark No. 1.	Why has water risen up in the bell-jar?	
7.	Phosphorus pentoxide is soluble in water.	What does it signify? Where has phosphorus pentoxide gone?	
8.	No more oxygen is present in the bell-jar now.	Absence of oxygen in the bell-jar can be tested by taking in burning match stick inside the bell-jar.	Air contains one part of oxygen and four parts of nitrogen. It is soluble in water.

CHAPTER 6

Science Laboratories

6.1 IMPORTANCE OF PRACTICAL WORK IN SCIENCE

No course in science can be considered as complete without including some practical work in it. The practical work is to be carried out by individual in a science laboratory. Most of the achievements of modern science are due to the application of the experimental method. At school stage practical work is even more important because of the fact that we 'learn by doing' scientific principles and applications are thus rendered more meaningful. It is a well known fact that an object handled impresses itself more firmly on the mind than an object merely seen from a distance or in an illustrations. Centuries of purely deductive work did not produce the some utilitarian results as a few decades of experimental work. Practical class room experiments help in broadening pupil's experience and develop initiative, resourcefulness and cooperation. Because of the reasons discussed above practical work forms a prominent feature in any science course.

6.2 ORGANISATION OF PRACTICAL WORK

Out of the various teaching methods discussed earlier the *Assignment method* is the only method that continues theory and practice in a harmonious manner and can be easily practiced in our schools. The *Heuristic method* is preeminently a *laboratory method*. However from this it should not be concluded that practical work in laboratory is impossible if the teacher. makes use of any other teaching method. Thus irrespective of the method adopted by the teacher for teaching of science in the class, practical work in laboratory must be attempted. The following guide lines will help the science teacher to make his practical work effective.

Guide Lines for Teachers

For smooth working in the laboratory teacher should give due consideration to the following points.

(*i*) If teacher follows the demonstration method to teach theory, he should remember the most important principle that practical work should go hand in hand with the theoretical work. Thus if a class is doing theoretical work in physics it should also do practical work in physics during the practical periods.

(*ii*) An attempt be made to arrange the practical work in such a way that each student is able to do his practical individually. Thus for practical work individual working be preferred in comparison to working in groups.

(*iii*) In case of a large class, it is convenient to divide the class in a suitable number of smaller groups, for practical work. A practical group in no case should have more than 20 students. The limit on practical group is essential otherwise teacher will not be able to devote individual attention to the students.

(*iv*) To save time on delivering a lecture about do's and don'ts in laboratory, card system is used. This card which contains certain amount of guidance printed on it is given to each pupil. In some laboratories where card system exists each student is given a card containing instructions about the experiment that he has to perform. This card also contains the details of the apparatus required. Student can complete his practical work according to instructions given in the card.

(*v*) The apparatus provided should be good so that students get an accurate result particularly in those experiments in which the student is likely to compare the numerical value of his result with some standard. However, every science teacher should gaurd against 'Cooking' of results by his pupil. If this bad habit of cooking is not checked in the beginning it persists through out the students' career.

(*vi*) A true and faithful record of each and every experiment be kept by pupils. The record should be complete in all respects.

(*vii*) To check the habit of 'cooking' teacher should see that students enter all their observations directly in their practical note book. The teacher should insist that the pupils do not go to the balance room without first entering the data in their note books.

(*viii*) Students should not be allowed to erase any figures. To change any wrong entry the same be crossed and correct figure entered only with the permission of the teacher.

(*ix*) Students should not be allowed to calculate results or write data on scrap papers.

(*x*) In practical note book the right hand page be reserved for record while the left hand page be left for diagram and calculations. This practice be followed for Assignment method.

For any other method the laboratory work be done on left hand page of practical note book and procedure etc. on right hand page of practical note book.

(*xi*) Teacher should see that students complete their practical note book in all respects and get it signed before they are allowed to leave the laboratory. Incomplete practical note books be kept in the laboratory and students be asked to complete it in their spare time.

(*xii*) Teacher should thoroughly check and critically examine the account written by students.

(*xiii*) Whenever a student is required to make use of a piece of apparatus for the first time it is the duty of the teacher to explain to his students the working of the apparatus. He should also explains reasons for necessary care and accuracy.

(*xiv*) Teacher should see that students find no difficulty to get apparatus and chemicals needed by them. In the absence of provision for laboratory assistants in our schools it is for the teacher that he arranges the apparatus in such a way that things frequently needed by students are easily accessible to them. Teacher should also emphasise proper and economical use of apparatus and chemicals.

(*xv*) While working with larger groups and with limited apparatus teacher can act as under:

(*a*) He may use assignment method.

(*b*) He may allow students to work in groups.

(*c*) He may devise alternate simple experiments and work with improvised apparatus.

(*d*) He may allow use of home made apparatus.

(*xvi*) Whenever the teacher is required to draw up suitable laboratory directions or instructions for practical work by pupils, be should keep the following points in mind:

(*a*) Beginner be given detailed directions.

(*b*) He should not tell the students what is actually going to happen.

(*c*) The main aim of the experiment should be made clear.

(*xvii*) During a practical class teacher should observe all children from his desk otherwise chances of accidents are there. Even when teacher has to move from his desk his power of control over the class should be such that students continue their work satisfactorily.

6.3 SCIENCE LABORATORIES

Combined Lecture room-cum-Laboratory

Laboratory is a spacious room where in a group of students carry out their practicals. The work of designing and building a science room (laboratory and lecture room) is that of the architect but science master should collaborate with the architect in planning for what is best from the educational point of view. The plan of a combined lecture room and laboratory for use in schools upto matriculation standard, devised by Dr. R.H. Whitehouse, formerly principal of the Central Training College, Lahore, has been adopted as the official standard plan by Punjab Education Department. The plan is shown in Fig. 6.1.

This plan combines laboratory and class room for science teaching. The suggested size of the room is 45′ X 25′ and it is meant for

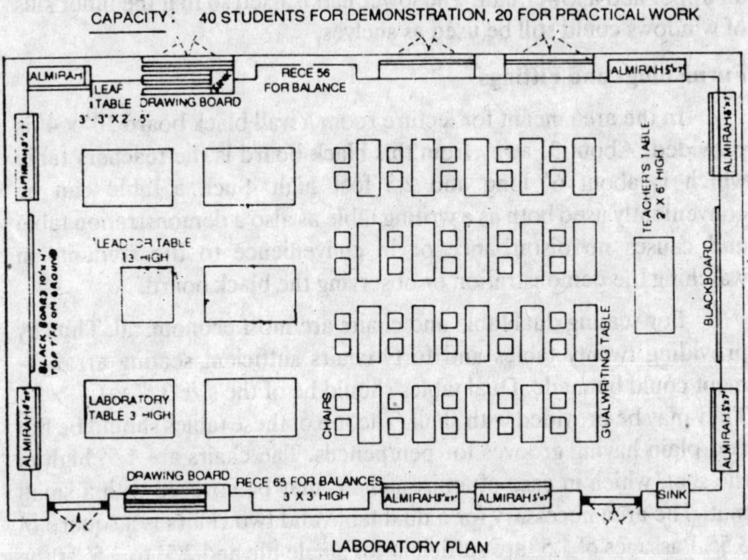

Fig. 6.1. Laboratory Plan.

a class of 40 students which is sub-divided in two groups of 20 each for practical work.

The size of the room is most economical. Though the length of the room is 45′ but it should not be considered as disadvantageous because the teacher is expected to address a class of 40 students who will be occupying only about half the room.

For constructing such a room walls are to be of 1′ 6" thick keeping Indian conditions in view, use of distemper be preferred to white wash for the walls. A perfectly smooth floor is preferable to one exhibiting any roughness. Such a floor is easier to clean of the two doors, one is used for lecture room and the other is reserved for laboratory part. To provide side lighting three large windows (6′ x 8′) are provided. One of these is provided near practical benches and two near seating accommodation. Doors as also windows should open outwards. The inner window sills may be used as shelves for carrying out experiments. To avoid flies wire gauze screens be provided to the windows. If necessary, in such a case, the windows be constructed with an upper and a lower half. The lower half is fixed so that the inner sills of windows could still be used as shelves.

Furnishings and Fittings

In the area meant for lecture room a wall black board 10′ x 4′ is provided. About 3′ away from this black board is the teachers table which is about 6′ long and 2.5 feet high. Such a table can be conveniently used both as a writing table as also a demonstration table and causes no disturbance or in convenience to the students in watching the demonstration or observing the black board.

For seating dual table and chairs are most economical. Thus by providing twenty tables and forty chairs sufficient seating arrangement could be made. Dual tables should be of the size 3.5′ x 1.5′ x 2′. They may be provided with shelf. The top of these tables should be flat and plain having grooves for pen/pencils. The chairs are 1.5′ high in the seat, which in case of an iron chair, may be covered with a small mat. The area necessary for a dual table and two chairs is a square of 3.5′. Passages of 1.5′ are sufficient for single file and 2.5′ to 3.5′ at the sides.

A sink is provided for use of the teacher. The size of the sink generally used is 18″ x 12″ x 6″.

The advantages of table and chair system are as under:

(*i*) They are quite economical.

(*ii*) They provide quite natural seats.

(*iii*) They allow enough space for easy passage of the students.

(*iv*) They can be easily moved while cleaning the room.

(*v*) They can be used for other purposes such as accommodating guests at various school functions.

Laboratory

In the laboratory part of the room are provided six laboratory tables which are made of wood and are perfectly plain. A black board is also provided on this side of the room. The laboratory tables are of the size 6′ x 3.5′ and are provided with a shelf on the working side just below the top. Four students can work on each table. The whole of each table except top should be stained dark. The top should be treated with wax ironed with a hot flat iron in order to fill the pores of the wood and to prevent the easy penetration of the liquids. The space between the tables and walls varies between 3′ and 4′ and passage-way at the end of the tables is 2′ wide. At school level the laboratory tables are not provided with any sink. Some of the reasons for not providing the sinks are as follows:

(*i*) *Economy:* A large economy is observed because much plumbing and a network of drains is avoided. Cost of sinks is also saved. For most of the experiments at school level a trough can serve the purpose.

(*ii*) *Usefulness:* The table is quite useful for both physics and chemistry. In absence of sinks more space is available for use as working space. Such a table can also be used for other purposes.

(*iii*) *Appearance and cleanliness:* The floor of the room is not broken for providing drains etc. It gives a better look.

(*iv*) *Tidiness:* The tables if provided with sink would make the room untidy because such tables invariably allow splashing of water which is likely to interfere with experiments and is likely to create problems.

As shown in the plan there are only three sinks, one for the teacher and two for the students. Of the two sinks for students one is placed in the window recess and the other in recess in the wall. Each of the sinks is provided with a drawing board having grooves arranged to drip over the sinks. It is used for placing beakers, flasks, etc. for drying.

For placing balances, recess in walls may be used. They may be about a foot wide at a height of about 3′, 3″. Such recess has the following advantages over wooden or stone shelf:

(*i*) It is very economical because only very small masonary is needed.

(*ii*) It is more substantial as compared to a bracket shelf.

(*iii*) It does not project into the room and so space economy can be made.

For providing ample accommodation for balances a length of 7′ to 7.5′ is sufficient.

In the plan provision has also been make for the storage of science apparatus, equipments etc. For this purpose there is a provision of eight almirahs (each with 7′ x 5′ dimensions). Each almirah is provided with shelves 1.5′ deep, of this 1′ is recessed in the wall and only 6″ projects out. These almirahs provided sufficient space for the storage of not only the apparatus, equipment etc. but can also serve the purpose of storage of science library.

Reagent shelves can be very conveniently placed on either side of the recesses for balances space can also be found, for placing notice boards for assignments of work, results of tests, etc., on the wall between the windows or just inside the doors.

Advantages

The combined lecture room-cum-laboratory discussed in previous pages has the following advantages:

(*i*) It is very economical.

(*ii*) It is compact and provides enough space for seating, working, storage etc.

(*iii*) It can be furnished easily and with meager resources.

(*iv*) It provides enough and comfortable seating space for the students.

(*v*) In this room science atmosphere prevails.

(*vi*) It provides an opportunity for better control. For a better control followings points be kept in view by a teacher.

(a) Every student has his assigned place which is indicated by his name written on a card placed in a brass card holder fixed on the leg of the table.

(b) The four boys working on any table be allotted number 1, 2, 3, 4 and number 1 of each table be asked to collect four sets of articles required for each table. Number 2 be asked to remove the dirty apparatus, after the period, to drain board and number 3 will remove clean apparatus. Number 4 will wipe down the table with a duster.

(c) Class monitors be named for cleaning dirty apparatus after school hours or during recess period.

(d) Students be made responsible for the correct alignment of their tables. For this black and white lines be pointed on the floor.

All Purpose Science Room

A special science room set aside for science facilities and materials is very desirable in an elementary school even where a self contained programme is conducted. This room can be specially planned in a new building, an unused class room, part of an art or shop room, or any other available space. This room can be used for special science projects, science equipment and supply storage, school green house, science fairs and exhibits. This room should contain the following if possible: running water, electrical outlets, working tables, a source of heat, work bench with assorted hand tools, several rolling carts for distribution of science materials and ample storage facilities.

This room will serve all aspects of general science work, both practical and theoretical but an effective teaching of special subjects may not be possible with this laboratory. The size of such a room convenient for 40 students is 45′ x 25′.

The elementary class room must serve the total elementary curriculum and so the plans be made in the regular class room for such science areas as *activity areas, storage areas, research and library areas, conference areas and display areas*.

Activity Areas

Most modern elementary class rooms contain much movable furniture. The centre of the room usually houses the movable desks or tables and chairs. The wall space areas provide opportunities for more stationary equipment and faculties. Science facilities be grouped as far as possible in one general area of the room. The needed equipment, supplies and other facilities should be readily and easily available for making, assembling, experimenting and demonstrating in science. This area should be well lighter, should contain running water if possible, electrical outlets and a source of heat. There should be an adequate space to work. When the room arrangement does not allow for work bench or table, it can be done on desks. The desk tops should be protected by laying sheets of card board, masonite or other suitable material.

Temporary work areas can be improvised by putting boards or plywood across two wooden boxes or saw horses. Schools can purchase standard work benches in any size to fit the age and size of the children who will use them.

Work Area Storage

By simply enclosing the bottom of a working bench, considerable storage area is made for construction supplies and hand tools. An attempt can be made to solve the storage problem by providing portable laboratory table or work bench that can be moved from room to room. Any table around school preferably 6′ x 6′ can be mounted on wheels. The lower level of the table can be used for the storage of supplies and equipment. Such tables are extremely useful because they can be moved out the way when space is needed

Same bench made more useful by boxing in the ends and back and adding a shelf or two inside.

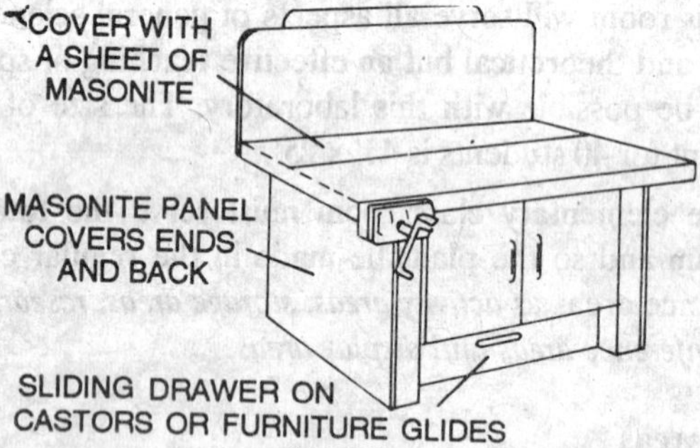

Fig. 6.2

Having one of these for each two rooms is extremely useful since they can be moved out of the way when the space is required. The custodian in the school could probably make a portable table within a couple of hours. The cost of converting such a table would be very little since the basic table would be available in the school. Occasionally parents can be asked to help with such projects.

Making Storage Cabinets

Storage space for a science programme can be improvised by using orange crates or other partitioned wooden boxes. Besides being either free or extremely inexpensive, the crates are easy to use as is shown. These boxes can be arranged side by side in a row along the wall in the science area. Casters could be attached to the bottom of the crates so that they could be moved around the room or from room to room. A piece of plywood attached to the back and extending over the top of the crate can supply display space. The possibilities for a variety

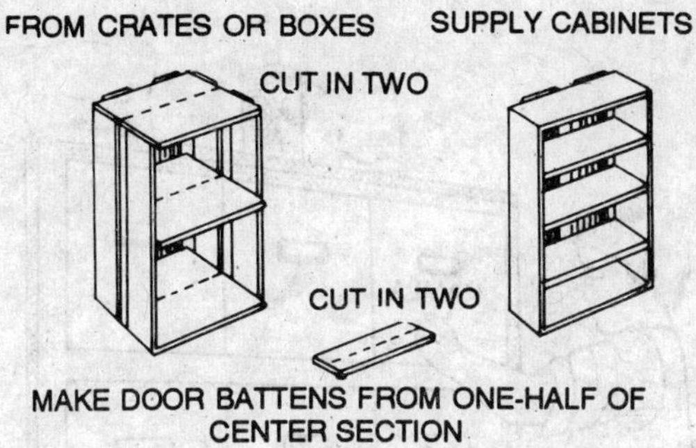

Fig. 6.3

Fig. 6.4

of user for these crates is limited only the ingenuity of the children and teachers.

Shoe Box Collection Storage

Shoe boxes provide devices for collecting and storing the readily available science maticular science area. For example, let us assume that the fifth class has just completed a science study of children collected bits of wire, bells, and light sockets; they made switches and telegraph sets. The teacher decided to put the collected magnetism and electricity materials in a shoe box with directions on how to make and use them as well as questions the children asked or solved. The teacher with the children's help did the same for other science curricular areas and eventually had many kits of materials for teaching science. Shoe boxes limit the amount of materials collected which makes the teacher more discriminating in selecting and storing materials. Plastic trays can be substituted for the shoe boxes.

Fig. 6.5

Classroom Research Corner

An area should be set aside for research from textbooks, charts, pamphlets, encyclopedias, and other reference books. A study area should be well-lighted, provided with adequate furniture – tables, chairs, book-shelves – and well-stocked with many kinds of supplementary science materials. Efforts should be made to include as wide a range as possible of reading levels and interests and areas of science. It should be a place where children can go for finding answers to some of their scientific questions. Encouragement should be provided by the teacher for stimulating the use of this area. The teacher can also point out to children that scientists, especially in large laboratories, also require great amounts of reading from these materials. Directions for use of the area should be worked out co-operately between the teacher and the students. Stress should be made on the use of many references and not upon just one source of information. The children can be encouraged to bring in science reading materials to add to the ever-growing science research corner.

Conference Area

There is very often need for the teacher and children to hold small conferences or carry on group planning in the science programme. An area can be set aside for this a purpose. Generally a table and six chairs is satisfactory if it is placed away from distracting influences. Occasionally the classroom research area can be as the conference area. Occasionally it merely means moving six chairs to the back of the room. However it is done, the conference area should allow small groups to confer and plan quietly without being disturbed or disturbing others.

Display Area

Bulletin boards and displays are essential tools for teaching science. They can arouse curiosity, stimulate interests, and raise questions. By doing so, these devices involve children in planning and developing the content and activities of the particular science study. Bulletin boards and display boards also provide all children with materials that may not be available in sufficient quantity. It can easily be seen that classrooms presenting science bulletin boards and display board places value and emphasis on science. This in itself is stimulating for children.

Construction of science display board and bulletin boards is the same as for any curricular area. By planning for such display board in advance, children and teachers can collect pictures, charts, models, and other materials long before they are required. Children, after working with the teacher, can assume much of the responsibility for the planning, collecting, and arranging of such display articles and bulletin boards.

List of common articles and apparatus is given below:

1. Microscope
2. Toothpicks
3. Tweezers
4. Optical lens
5. Euglena
6. Microscope slides
7. Test tube rack
8. Jar

9. Cover glass
10. Dropper
11. Iodine stain
12. Methylene blue
13. Rosin
14. Kosher salt
15. Brown sugar
16. Pond water culture
17. Paramecium caudatum
18. Soda straw balance
19. Amoeba proteus
20. Calcium chloride
21. Sugar
22. Calcium chloride
23. Straws
24. Empty bottle
25. Molasses
26. Vinegar
27. Coffee tin lid
28. Hotplate
29. Yeast
30. Measuring cup
31. Meas. spoons
32. Vegetables
33. Spoon
34. Knife
35. Weeds
36. Test tubes
37. Bottle brush

6.4 LABORATORY PLANNING FOR SENIOR SECONDARY SCHOOLS

In a senior secondary school the arrangements are made to provide education in physics, chemistry and biology as elective subjects in addition to teaching of general science. In senior secondary school a provision has to be made for four laboratories, one each for physics, chemistry, biology and general science. The laboratories in senior secondary schools are almost the same as in colleges. Each laboratory is provided with a preparation-cum-store room attached to it. The size of the laboratory will depend on the number of students likely to work in it at a time. About 30 sq. ft. space be provided for each student. The structural details are generally provided by the architects but the following points be kept in mind.

Planning

It would be better if science teacher is consulted and for this there should be frequent conferences between the science teacher and the architect. Various points be thoroughly discussed. Some of the points of consideration are as under:

(*i*) Laboratories and class rooms should not be mixed on the same corridor.

(*ii*) Laboratories be situated, as far as possible, away from crafts room, music room, play fields, main gate etc.

(*iii*) The consideration be given to proximity of stores, preparation room, balance room, green houses etc.

Following points be given due consideration while planning individual laboratories

(*i*) Each student is easily accessible to the teacher.

(*ii*) There is minimum of movement.

(*iii*) Each student has a cupboard, bottles, heating point and a sink near him.

(*iv*) Teacher can easily watch each student.

(*v*) Black board is visible to each student.

(*vi*) Each student can easily see the demonstration.

(*vii*) There is enough space (4.5′) between two laboratory tables.

(*viii*) Master switches be provided to control electricity, gas, water etc. in each laboratory.

Lighting

Proper lighting arrangements be made for laboratory tables and class rooms. Special attention be given to the lighting of demonstration table and black board. It would be preferred if a provision could be made for electrical lights over tables through pulleys so that their height may be varied from 2 to 8 ft. Two way switches be provided for controlling the main lighting from doors and preparation rooms. Dark blinds or curtain must be provided for each laboratory.

Ventilation

It possible each laboratory should be surrounded by a 6′ verandah on all sides to keep away the direct heat of the sun. Ventilators be provided as usual. In case of chemistry laboratory ceiling should be high and exhaust fans must be provided

For laboratory ventilation full height windows are desirable. To avoid direct draughts even when the windows are open windows should be designed as under.

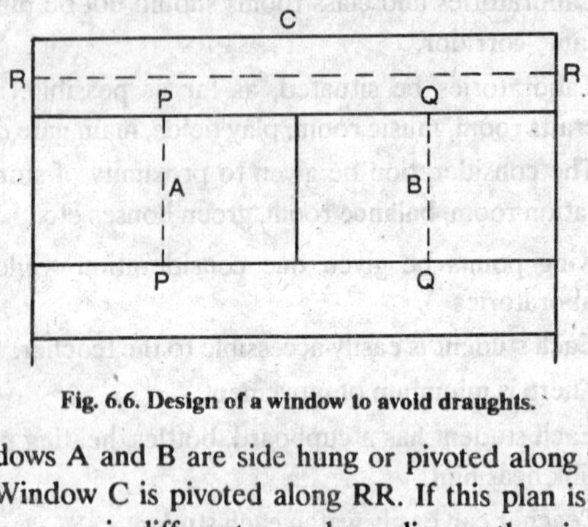

Fig. 6.6. Design of a window to avoid draughts.

Windows A and B are side hung or pivoted along the axis PP and QQ. Window C is pivoted along RR. If this plan is used them windows can open in different ways depending on the wind direction. In dark room the ventilation can be provided by deflecting incoming and outgoing air by opaque partition. A no door arrangement as shown on next page may be made.

Water Supply

Provision of water supply must be made in every laboratory. Water supply is most essential item and for this purpose proper arrangement of water taps and sinks is a must in every laboratory. In case of non-availability of adequate water supply from municipal/local

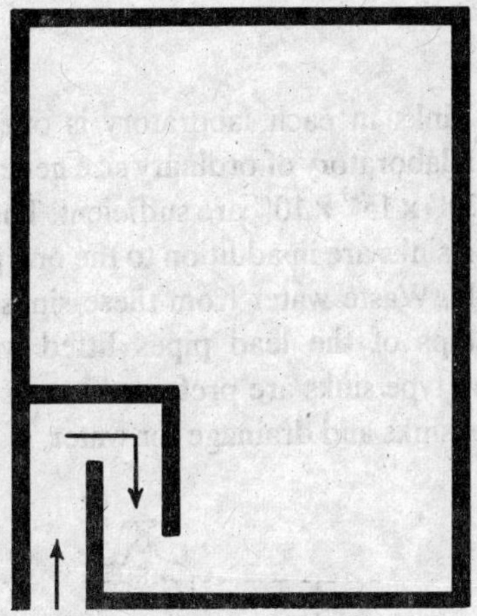

Fig. 6.7. A 'no-door' Dark Room

sources alternate arrangements have to be made. For making alternate arrangements suggestion given below be considered.

A water storage tank having a capacity of 1000 to 5000 litres be constructed with concrete and cement or a readymade tank of synthetic material be purchased and such a tank be then placed at the roof of the room. Water be then lifted using electric pump for filling this tank. The water supply is then provided from this storage tank to the laboratories. A tentative scheme for storage and supply of water is shown in Fig. 6.8.

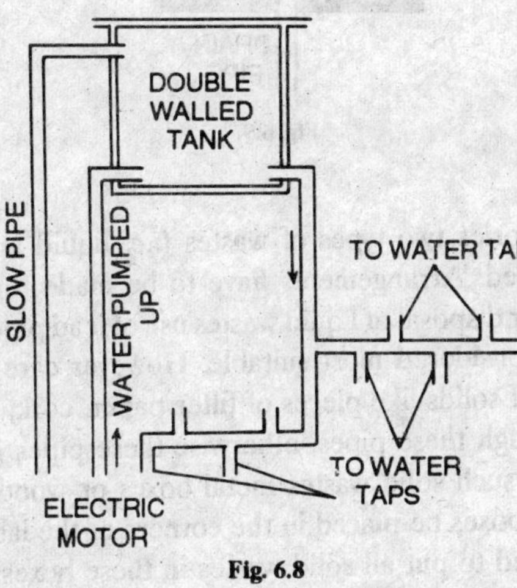

Fig. 6.8

Sinks

Provision of sinks in each laboratory is one of the essential requirements. For a laboratory of ordinary size generally four sinks of 15″ x 12″ x 8″ or 20″ x 15″ x 10″ are sufficient. These sinks be fitted on side walls. These sinks are in addition to the one provided with the demonstration table. Waste water from these sinks is carried to the drains with the helps of the lead pipes fitted with the sinks. In laboratories kitchen type sinks are preferred to wash basin type. Fig. 6.9 gives a sketch of sinks and drainage for water.

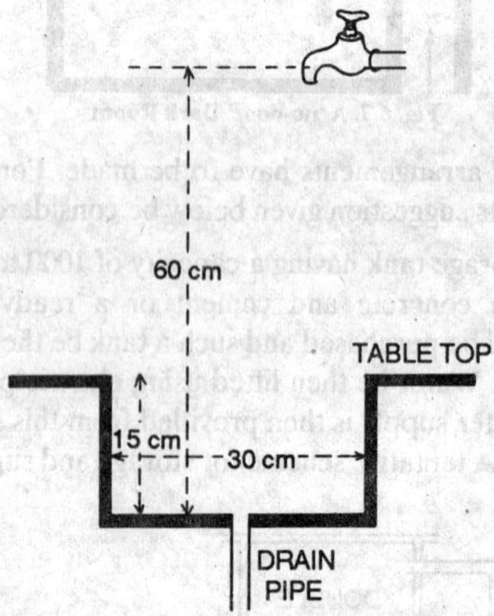

Fig. 6.9

Waste Disposal

In laboratories two types of wastes (*i.e.* liquid and solid) are often encountered. Arrangements have to be made for disposal of these wastes. For disposal of liquid wastes use of lead pipes or earthen ware pipes is considered most suitable. However care be taken to avoid the flow of solids like pieces of filter paper, cork, broken glass pieces etc. through these pipes, otherwise these pipes get chocked. For disposal of such solid wastes metal boxes or wooden boxes be provided. Such boxes be placed in the corners of the laboratory and students be asked to put all solid wastes in these boxes. Such waste boxes can even be placed under the sinks as shown in Fig. 6.10.

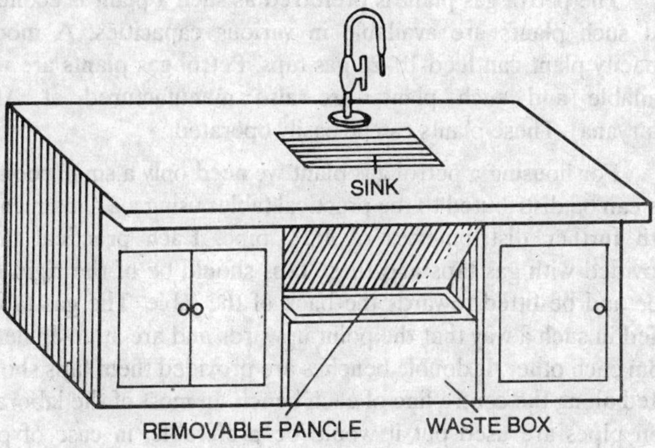

Fig. 6.10. A space saving position of a disposal box

Pipe Lines

Installation of water pipes and gas pipes is another important aspect for furnishing a science laboratory. While installing pipes some of the points that be given due consideration are given below:

(*i*) Not more than 4 or 5 half inches pipes be led from any 1″ pipe for purpose of supply of water or drainage of water.

(*ii*) In case of physics laboratory all efforts be made to avoid iron pipes.

(*iii*) Pipes should never be placed on the laboratory tables.

(*iv*) It is convenient if the pipe fittings are not underground.

Gas Supply

For adequate supply of fuel gas to the laboratory generally any one of the following arrangements is made.

(*i*) Kerosene oil gas plant is installed.
(*ii*) Coal gas plant is installed.
(*iii*) Petrol gas plant is installed.
(*iv*) Gobar gas plant is installed.

The petrol gas plant is preferred as such a plant is economical and such plants are available in various capacities. A moderate capacity plant can feed 10–20 gas taps. Petrol gas plants are readily available and such plants are also manufactured at Ambala (Haryana). These plants can be easily operated.

For housing a petrol gas plant we need only a small room. The gas can be distributed to the practical tables using a 2″ main gas pipe with further distributeries of 1/2″ pipe. Each practical table is provided with gas taps and these taps should be of the rigid nozzle type and be fitted towards the back of the table. The gas tables be fitted in such a way that the point upwards and are at an angle of 45° from each other. If double benches are provided them taps should be fitted along the centre line of each bench. In most of the laboratories iron pipes are used but it would be preferable, in case of physics laboratory, if we use brass pipes. For controlling the supply of gas in addition to main control valve provision be made to control the supply of gas to each group of tables. These controls should be easily accessible to teacher and should not be easily accessible to students.

Laboratory Tables

The provision of laboratory tables as a must for each laboratory. The taps of laboratory tables be preferably made of teak wood. However other hard wood such as sheesham or deodar can also be used for making tops of laboratory tables. These tops are generally 1″ thick. Other parts of the table *i.e.* legs, drawers etc. may be made of any other type of locally available wood. Plywood or hardboard can also be used for drawers. In physics laboratory tables without drawers are preferred but in chemistry laboratory such drawers are provided with the laboratory tables.

In addition to these provision for boards be made in the laboratories. For this either wall black boards be provided or movable wooden black boards with stands can be used.

The organisation of laboratories in secondary schools was also discussed at a seminar (All India) on the teaching of science in secondary schools. This seminar was held at Tara Devi (Simla) and it made some recommendations. Its recommendations under various heads are given below.

Lay out

(a) Provision be made for one general science laboratory and one laboratory for each of the three elective subjects *i.e.* physics, chemistry and biology, in every higher secondary school.

(b) A floor space of 30 sq ft per student be provided in each laboratory.

(c) Adjacent store room be provided with each laboratory.

(d) A part of store room may be earmarked for use as a preparation room.

(e) In science wing, some suitable place for work benches with tools, be provided.

(f) A minimum of two class rooms provided with galleried seats be provided in each school.

Equipment

The list of equipment for each laboratory as recommended at the Tara Devi (Simla) seminar is given below:

Science Room

Science room should be provided with

(*i*) Galleried seats

(*ii*) One demonstration table (8′ × 4′) having cupboards, gas and water fittings.

(*iii*) A black board or wall board.

(*iv*) Black curtains for covering doors, windows and ventilators.

General Science Laboratory

It must have the following equipment:

(*i*) Working tables (ordinary) with drawers.

(*ii*) Demonstration table (8′ × 4′) provided with gas and water points.

(*iii*) A minimum of two sinks be provided in the corners of the laboratory.

(*iv*) A wall board or black board.
(*v*) Stools (in two sizes).
(*vi*) Almirahs (wooden or steel).

Chemistry Laboratory

The equipment for chemistry laboratory is as under:

(*i*) Almirahs (wooden and steel).
(*ii*) Wall board or black board.
(*iii*) Demonstration table (8′ x 4′) with cupboards, water and gas points.
(*iv*) Working tables with cupboards, shelves, water and gas points.
(*v*) Balance room should be attached to the laboratory.
(*vi*) Sinks on each working table or at least two large sinks at the corners of the laboratory.
(*vii*) A fume cupboard.
(*viii*) A wooden box half filled with sand for use as waste material box.
(*ix*) Acid proof drainage system.
(*x*) Shelves for reagent bottle on each working table and wall shelves for storage of reagent bottles.

Physics Laboratory

Physics laboratory should have the following equipment:

(*i*) Working tables (ordinary) with teak wood top.
(*ii*) At least one table having gas point fitted to it. This may be used for experiments on heat.
(*iii*) Projected platforms for balances.
(*iv*) Almirahs.
(*v*) Demonstration table having drawers, water and gas points.
(*vi*) Wall board or black board.
(*vii*) Two large sinks at the corners of the laboratory.
(*viii*) Stools (in two sizes).
(*ix*) Physics laboratory should have an attached dark room.

Biology Laboratory

Biology laboratory should be equipped with the following:

(*i*) Tables (6′ x 2′ x 2.5′) with water fittings and drawers.

(*ii*) Two sinks at the corners of the laboratory

(*iii*) Almirahs

(*iv*) Stools (in two sizes)

(*v*) Wall board or black board

(*vi*) Small table racks.

(*vii*) Wall shelves.

(*viii*) A froggery, where necessary

Special attention be paid to lighting arrangement in biology laboratory. It should have glass panes on the northern side and pendant lights over the tables.

General

Store rooms attached with the laboratories should be well equipped with almirahs, racks, sink etc. For storage of inflammable and poisonous substances separate shelter be provided.

In schools having larger number of students a provision be made for separate workshop which should have work benches and tool cabinet. However in smaller schools a few work benches may be placed in science wing.

Provision of a first aid and fire extinguishing apparatus be made near each laboratory. Arrangements for water supply and gas supply to each laboratory must also be made.

Administration

Each laboratory be under the supervision of a laboratory attendant. Attendants for laboratories be persons having middle school qualifications. Each school should also be provided with two store-keeper-cum-laboratory assistants and the minimum qualifications for persons to be appointed as store-keeper-cum-laboratory assistant be matriculation. If there are many work shops in a school and if there is enough work then a mechanic way also be provided to the school.

For conduct of practicals in physics, chemistry and biology, each of these subjects be allotted at least two consecutive periods during a week. An effort be made to provide apparatus and equipment so that each students can complete his experiment individually. However if enough material resources are not available then students may be asked to do the practicals in groups. A group should not be of more than two students in case of practicals for physics, chemistry and biology and must not exceed a limit of three for practicals in general science.

If cards for each experiment are prepared then it would help and facilitate the work in a practical class.

Some do's and don'ts for the laboratories be made clear to the students. They should be asked to complete their practical note-book before they leave the laboratory. Teacher should maintain a date wise record of each student.

Plans for laboratories

(*i*) Physics

(*ii*) Chemistry

(*iii*) Biology

(*iv*) General Science

6.5 LABORATORY INSTRUCTIONS

Instructions to Pupils

When a group comes to laboratory for practical work it should be given a guidance for the experiment to be performed. Such guidance can be given by (*i*) Laboratory instructions (*ii*) Laboratory manuals or (*iii*) Instruction cards.

(*i*) Laboratory Instructions

Laboratory instructions should be given in a clear and simple language. It should give a precise but systematic method of performing the experiment. Special emphasis be given on how the record is to be kept and number of observations to be taken. Calculations be clearly explained and precautions to be observed be specifically emphasised.

(*ii*) Laboratory Manuals

Any good laboratory manual should contain the following.

(a) It should contain full and complete directions about the experiment. Such directions should clearly give the procedure to be followed and the precautions to be observed.

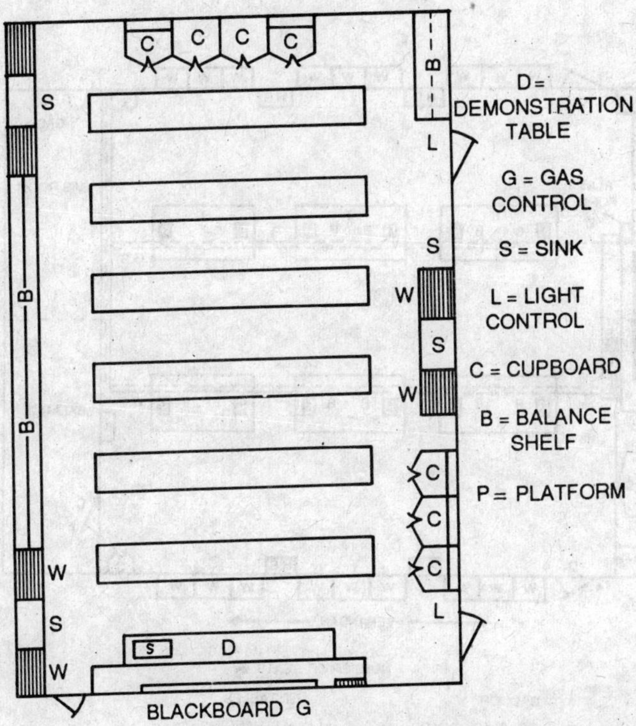

Fig. 6.11. A Physics Laboratory

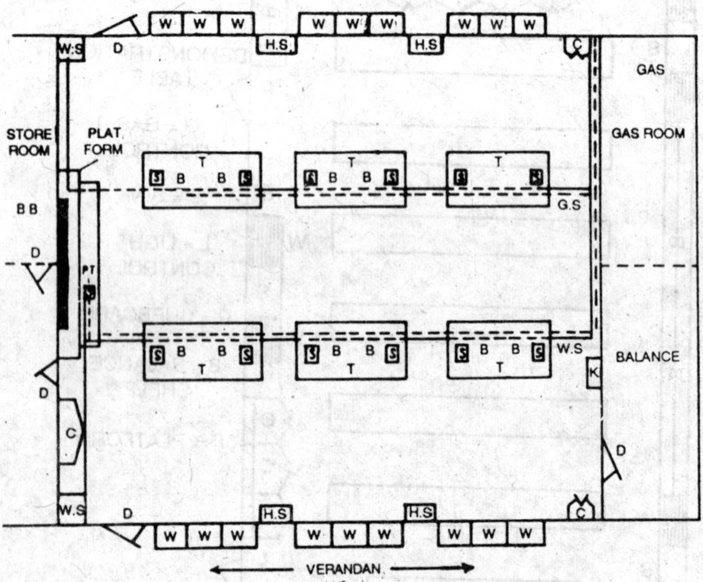

NUMBER OF SEATS: 24

D: DOOR.

B.B: BLACK BOARD

PT: PLATFORM

W.S: WALL SINK

D.T: DEMONSTRATION TABLE.

S: SINK

B: BURNERS.

T: TABLES.

H.S: HANGING WALL SHELVES.

G.S: WATER SUPPLY PIPES.

C: CUPBOARDS

K: KIPPS (APPARATUS) GAS STAND.

F.C : MUME CHAMBER.

Fig. 6.12. A Chemistry Laboratory

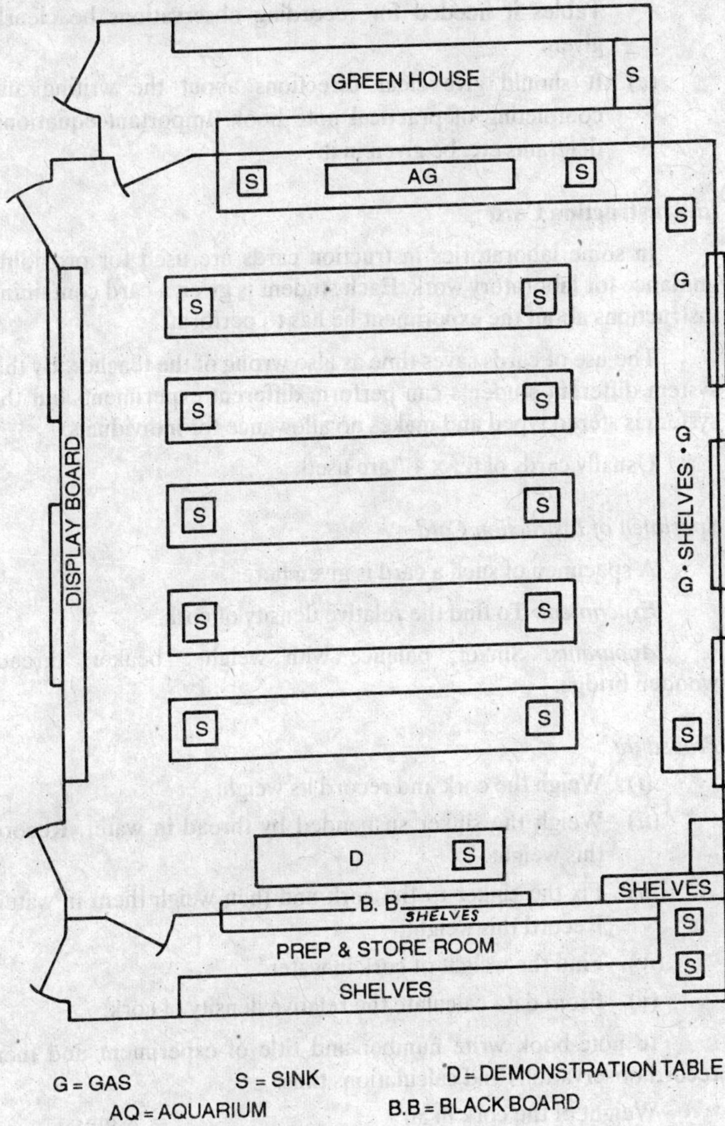

Fig. 6.13. A Biology Laboratory

(b) It should give the method of recording of observations. Tables if needed for recording observations be clearly given.

(c) It should give clear directions about the writing and completing of practical note book. Important equations, diagrams etc. be given in it.

(*iii*) Instruction Card

In some laboratories instruction cards are used for providing guidance for laboratory work. Each student is given a card containing instructions about the experiment he has to perform.

The use of cards saves time as also wrong of the teacher. By this system different students can perform different experiments but the system is stereo typed and makes no allowance for individuals.

Usually cards of 6″ x 4″ are used.

Specimen of Instruction Card

A specimen of such a card is given here:

Experiment: To find the relative density of cork.

Apparatus: Sinker, balance with weights, beaker, thread, wooden bridge.

Procedure

(*i*) Weigh the cork and record its weight.

(*ii*) Weigh the sinker suspended by thread in water. Record this weight.

(*iii*) Fix the sinker to the cork and then weigh them in water. Record this weight.

(*iv*) Find the weight of cork in water.

(*v*) From data calculate the relative density of cork.

In note-book write number and title of experiment and then record observations and calculations thus:

Weight of the cork in air = X gms.

Weight of the sinker in water = Y gms.

Weight of the cork and the sinker in water = Z gms.

$\therefore$ Weight of the cork in water $= (Z - Y) = p$ gms.

Weight of water equal in volume to the cork $= (X - p) = Q$ gms.

$$\text{Relative density of cork} = \frac{\text{Weight of the cork}}{\text{Weight of equal volume of waer}}$$

$$\text{Relative density of cork} = \frac{X}{X-p} \text{ or } \frac{X}{Q}$$

$$= \text{.........................}$$

6.6 PUPILS PRACTICAL NOTE BOOKS

For keeping a true and faithful record of practical work done by him each pupil is required to have a practical note book. An effort be made to avoid printed note books and plain note books be encouraged. By using plain note books teacher can make his students to follow any suitable method of keeping record of the experiment.

As a general practice description is given on the right hand page and observations are recorded on the left hand page. In case assignment method is used them the left hand page is reserved for preparatory work and laboratory record is kept on right hand page which contains description as also the observations.

The record of the method should be brief and in the first person singular. A three column system be used for keeping a record of experiments about the properties of gases etc. The three column be headed *Experiment, Observation* and *Inference*.

The precautions that have been observed while performing the experiment be recorded at the end in the first person singular (past tense).

All records in practical note book be made with black lead pencil. The diagrams should be simple and will labelled.

6.7 COMMON ACCIDENTS AND THEIR REMEDIES

Burns

Burns by Dry Heat (i.e. by flame, hot objects etc.). For slight burns apply *Burnol* and *Sarson oil*.

In case of blisters caused by burns apply *Burnol* at once and rush to dispensary.

Caution. *Heat burns should never be washed.*

Acid Burns

Wash with water and then with a saturated solution of sodium bicarbonate and finally with water. Even after this if burning persists, wipe the skin dry with cotton wool and apply *Sarson oil* and *Burnol*.

Caution. In case of conc. sulphuric acid, wipe it from the skin before giving the above treatment.

Alkali Burns

Wash with water and then with 1% acetic acid and finally with water. Dry the skin and apply *Burnol*.

Cuts

In case of a minor cut allow it to bleed for a few seconds and remove the glass piece if any. Apply a little methylated spirit or *Dettol* on the skin and cover with a piece of leucoplast.

For serious cuts call the Doctor at once. In the mean while try to stop bleeding by applying pressure above the cut. The pressure should not be continued for more than five minutes.

Note. Minor bleeding can be stopped easily by applying concentrated ferric chloride solution or alum.

Eye Accidents

Acid in Eye. At once wash the eye with water a number of times. Then wash it with 1% sodium carbonate solution by means of an eye-glass.

Alkali in Eye. At once wash with water and then with 1% boric acid solution by means of an eye-glass.

Foreign Particles in Eye. Do not rub the eye. Wash it by sprinkling water into the eye. Open the eye and remove the particle by means of a clean handkerchief or cotton wool. Again wash freely with water.

Poisons

If a solid or liquid goes to the mouth, but is not *swallowed*, spit it at once and repeatedly rinse with water. If the mouth is scalded, apply olive oil or *ghee*.

Acids. Dilute by drinking much water or preferably milk of magnesia.

Caustic Alkalies. Dilute by drinking water and then drink a glass of lemon or orange juice.

Arsenic of Mercury Compounds. Immediately give an emetic *e.g.* One table spoon full of salt or zinc sulphate is a tumbler of warm water.

Inhalation of Gases

Pungent gases like chlorine, sulphur dioxide, bromine vapours etc. When inhaled in large quantities often choke the throat and cause suffocation. In such a case remove the victim to the open air and loosen the clothing at the neck. The patient should inhale dilute vapours of ammonia or gargle with sodium bicarbonate solution.

Fire

Burning clothing. It clothes have caught fire then lay the victim on the floor and wrap a fire-proof blanket tightly around him. The fire in the burning clothes will thus be extinguished. *Never throw water on the person* as it will cause serious boils on his body.

Burning Reagents. In case of fire on the working table at once turn out the gas taps and remove all things which are likely to ignite. Following methods be used to extinguish the fire.

(*i*) If any liquid in a beaker or flask has caught fire, cover the mouth of the vessel with a clean clamp cloth or duster.

(*ii*) Most of the fire on the working table can be extinguished by throwing sand on them.

(*iii*) If any wooden structure has caught fire it is put up by throwing water on it.

(*iv*) *Never throw water on burning oil or spirit*. Since it will only spread the fire. Throwing of a mixture of sand and sodium bicarbonate on the fire is most effective.

6.8 FIRST AID BOX

A first aid box should be provided in every laboratory. It should contain the following materials.

Bandages (3-4 rolls of different sizes), gauze, lint, cotton wool, leucoplast.

A pair of forceps, a pair of scissors, safety pins.

Glass dropper, two eye-glasses.

Vaseline, boric acid powder, sodium bicarbonate powder, a tube of Burnol.

Sarson oil, olive oil, glycerine

Picric acid solution, Tannic acid solution 1% acetic acid, 1% boric acid, 1% sodium bicarbonate, saturated solution of sodium carbonate.

Methylated spirit, rectified spirit, Dettol.

CHAPTER 7

Apparatus and Equipment

7.1 INTRODUCTION

Procuring of adequate and right type of apparatus is one of the most important aspect of science teaching since the funds at the disposal of science master are only limited so he has to be very judicious in expending it. Thus a lot of planning is needed before making actual purchases.

7.2 PLANNING

Teacher should be very careful while planning the purchase of equipment for the laboratory. He should carefully weigh each item to be purchased with its educational worth. He may classify his requirements as under:

(*i*) Apparatus required for laboratory work.

(*ii*) Apparatus required for demonstration purposes.

(*iii*) Apparatus required for general use.

While determining the quantity of apparatus to be purchased, he should keep the following points in mind.

(*i*) Financial resources at his disposal.

(*ii*) Demonstration and laboratory work that has to be done during the year.

(*iii*) Scheme of work including the method of teaching to be used.

(*iv*) Storage facilities available.

Before making actual purchases a list be prepared of experiments to be informed by students and principles to be demonstrated by the teacher. For demonstration only one set will do but for experiments to be carried out by the students the member of sets required will be equal to the member of students working at a time. Some additional sets be purchased to cover up for the breakages etc. only such articles which are really required should be purchased.

If only limited funds are available them the purchases of beakers, flaskes, funnels, files etc. should be accorded first priority. These are the articles which are required by students while doing experiments. When ample store of such articles has been made them only the apparatus needed for demonstration be purchased. If funds are available articles such as camera, magic lantern, models etc. may be purchased. Another important point which must be considered is that there is enough accommodation for the proper storage of articles likely to be purchased. While ordering for purchases scheme of things; method of teaching and knowledge and ability of teacher must also be given due consideration.

Keeping in view the points discussed above the teacher should prepare a list of articles to be purchased. While selecting apparatus teacher must not be tempted by attractive descriptions given in catalogue. While preparing an indent the teacher should give full specifications of the article required. In the absence of such specifications it is just possible that you make purchase of items which you never intended to purchase. For selecting a good firm the list of apparatus with complete specification be sent to some competing and reputed firms and they be asked to quote their lowest rates. A specimen for inviting quotation in shown below.

S. No.	*Artilces*	*Quality*	*Size*	*Quantity*
1.	R.B. flasks	Pyrex glass	250 ml	10 doz.
2.	Titration flasks	Pyrex glass	100 ml	10 doz.
3.	Troughs	Pneumatic glass	12" dia	2 doz.
4.	Nitric acid	Commercial		5 l
5.	Sulphuric acid	B.D.H.		1 l

After receiving quotations a reliable firm quoting the lowest rate be asked to make the supplies.

The UNESCO designed apparatus for tropical schools is very satisfactory. The government of India is considering an arrangement for the manufacture of such instruments and making supplies of these to schools in lies of cash grants.

Science master should carefully check the items received and then arrange them properly after making entries in the stock register.

7.3 ARRANGEMENT AND CARE

The apparatus received be arranged in almirahs provided with glass fronts and preferably be fitted with mortise locks to avoid dust getting in. Apparatus should be arranged in such a way that each and every item could be easily located. Items which are frequently required be stored at such places that they are readily available. The apparatus should be arranged one deep of shelf; several rows of same articles may be placed on one shelf. The apparatus may be arranged either subject wise or alphabetically. If we arrange the apparatus subject wise we find that some articles fall under more than one heading and if we arrange them alphabatically we find that glass and metal articles are coming together in which there is more likely hood of breakage. Thus it is always better to reserve a few almirahs for apparatus required for individual practical work in which the apparatus be arranged alphabetically. The chemicals can also be stored alphabetically.

A list be pasted on the almirahs showing the names of articles stored in it.

The apparatus needed only for demonstration purposes may be stored in separate almirahs subject wise.

Chemicals can be stored even on open shelves. For this purpose two open shelves can be provided on either side of the recess for balances. However dangerous and costly chemicals like phosphorus or sodium or salts of mercury, bismith or cadmium be stored separately in an almirah. The containers or bottles containing chemicals should be neatly labelled.

To effect economy in space some items of common use such as stands, holders, clamps etc. many be stored outside almirahs. Two possible arrangements for storage of iron stands are shown on next page.

Care of Equipment and Apparatus

Care of equipment and apparatus is one of the important functions of the science master. For this the apparatus kept in

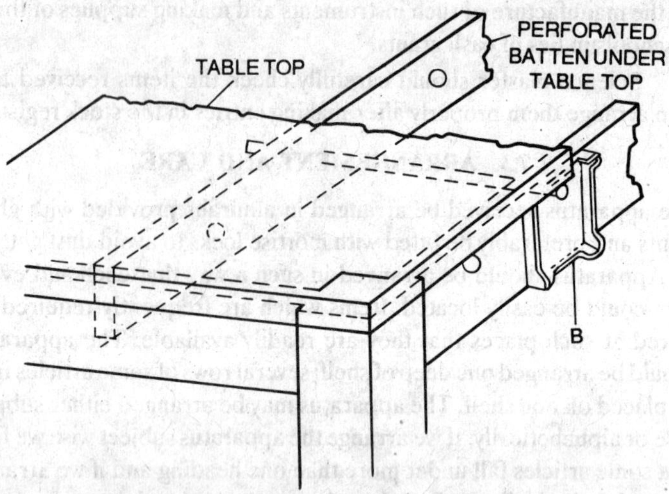

Fig. 7.1. Method of storing iron stands under a table top. A—base of stand.

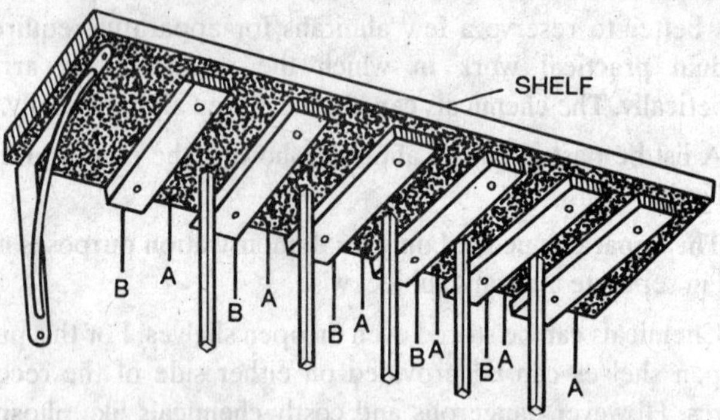

Fig. 7.2. Another method of storing iron stands under a shelf
A–base of stand B—slotted batten

almirahs must be checked at regular intervals. During this checking operation the apparatus should not only be inspected but it should also be dusted, cleaned and polished if necessary. If proper care is taken the life of the apparatus will increase. For proper upkeep and maintenance the following points be kept in mind.

(*i*) After use the apparatus should be properly cleaned before it is returned to its proper place. Never return dirty apparatus to its proper place. This is specially applicable in case of glass apparatus used in chemistry laboratory. For proper cleaning of glass articles we can make use of soap, pumice stone, hot alkali solution, acidified potassium dichromate solution etc.

(*ii*) For cleaning items made of brass we can use *Brasso*. *Brasso* be applied to the article with finger covered with a piece of muslin, allowed to dry and then rubbed off with a clean duster.

(*iii*) Iron articles are generally polished. For polishing such articles use Black Japan thinned with a little turpentine of kerosene oil. Aluminium paint can also be used. If the article to be painted has any rust it should be removed, by rubbing with an emery paper, before painting the article. Use of kerosene oil can also be made for removal of rust. Take care to apply vaseline on screws and hinges of iron articles during rainy season.

(*iv*) Wooden articles be left in the sun after being polished with spirit polish. Spirit polish can be made by dissolving shellac in methylated spirit. One or two coatings of it are them applied on the article.

(*v*) The top of each laboratory table is unpolished but it should be waxed (specially in case of chemistry laboratory) to avoid the action of acids. For waxing either paraffin wax or candles can be used. Wax is coated over the table with the help of painters brush and is then spread over and smoothened using the hot iron of washerman. It is then allowed to dry and any excess of wax is scarped off with a blunt knife. It is then polished with a coarse duster.

(*vi*) Special attention be paid to keep sinks clean. For cleaning sinks use *vein* powder or some other cleaning powder. Use special chemicals for removal of stains if they persist.

(*vii*) In chemistry laboratory special attention be paid to the fact that stoppers of bottles are not lost or get changed. For this they should be tagged to the bottle either using a copper wire or a rubber band.

(*viii*) The apparatus which is frequently used by students may go out of its proper adjustment and a good science master must find time for its proper adjustment and must also be able to carry out minor repairs. For this the science room must be equipped with a tool kit containing usual hammer, wrenches, pliers, screw drivers, forceps etc.

(*ix*) Glass panes of almirahs should also be cleaned occasionally. For cleaning glass panes use monkey brand soap. Rub a wet sponge over the soap and then over the pane and clean off with a duster. Pumice stone dipped in water is in methylated spirit and rubbed over the panes will remove all dirt.

(*x*) For cleaning of glass apparatus in general and burette and pipette in particular use a solution of potassium dichromate acidified with dilute sulphuric acid.

7.4 RECORD

Maintaince of a proper record of the apparatus, material etc. in the laboratory is one of the important duties of the science master. For this after receipt of articles they should be thoroughly checked and then they be entered in the stock register. A specimen page from a stock register is shown on next page.

Seperate stock register be maintained for consumable and non-consumable items, permanent articles, glass articles etc. Following stock registers are generally maintained in schools.

(*i*) Stock register for non-breakable articles.

(*ii*) Stock register for breakable articles.

(*iii*) Stock register for consumable articles.

(*iv*) Stock register for permanent articles.

In addition to various stock registers following registers should also be maintained.

(i) Order Register

This Register is meant for orders sent for the purchase of new apparatus. Entries in this register should indicate the serial number and date of the order, name of the firm to whom the order has been placed, details of articles ordered, articles received, cost of articles

Page........

Specimen Page from

Stock Register

Stock Register of.....................................Department
Name of the article...............................

Month & Date	*Particulars (Name of the Firm, Bill No. and Date)*	*Receipt*			*Consumed/ written of*		*Balance*		*Initials of Tr. incharge*	*Remarks*
		Qty.	*Rate*	*Amount*	*Qty.*	*Amount*	*Qty.*	*Amount*		

received. For convenience a copy of the order be posted on the left hand page of this register and a copy of supply under be pasted on the right hand page.

(ii) Requirement Register

This register if maintained makes the task of placing orders easier. Teacher will enter in this register the items whose absence is felt by the teacher at the time of demonstration of an experiment or during the practical class. If such entries are not made them there is every likelihood that some of the items needed by the teacher may be left out while placing the order for purchase of material and equipment. The requirement register should invariably be consulted by the teacher whenever be places orders for the purchase of materials or other requirements of the laboratory.

(iii) Stock Register for Science Club

Organising science clubs is quite useful in creating a scientific atmosphere and each secondary school is expected to have a science club. For organising various activities of science club the teacher needs different types of apparatus, equipment and materials. It is desirable to maintain a separate stock register for the science club. In this register all the apparatus meant for science club be entered. Entries of models, charts and collections made by students should also be made in this register.

Maintenance of Stock Registers. Following points should be given done consideration while maintaining any stock register:

(*i*) The outer cover of the stock register should indicate the name of the register, name of the school, date of opening and closing of the register, etc.

(*ii*) A certificate be given on the first page of the register indicating the total number of pages in the register. All the pages be numbered serially and the above certificate be countersigned by the head of the institution.

(*iii*) Either seperate stock registers be maintained or the same stock register be divided into a number of portions under various heads such as Mechanics, Heat, Light, Sound, Electricity, Magnetism etc.

(*iv*) An effort be made to make entries alphabetically.

(*v*) An Index be given at the beginning of the stock register.

(*vi*) Each receipt entry should be entered with date of receipt and the items consumed or broken be shown in the columns meant for this purpose. All these entries be initialled by science teacher and countersigned by head of institution.

7.5 HOME MADE APPARATUS

It is expected that science teacher is capable of devising and making apparatus for some simple experiments, modify apparatus and carry out simple repairs. *The apparatus devised and made in school work shop or laboratory by the teacher or students is known as home-made apparatus*. A science teacher with a little thought and ingenuity can make a number of valuable and serviceable models making use of cheap materials such as Jam-Jars, bits of wire, corks, motor parts etc. Some of the advantages of using home-made apparatus are as under:

(*i*) Such an apparatus is economical.

(*ii*) Use of such an apparatus makes more obvious the application of science to life and things around us.

(*iii*) It provides an encouragement to the student to make such an apparatus and adopt it as a hobby.

(*iv*) It helps to correlate science with manual training.

(*v*) It creates extra interest in the subject.

(*vi*) It provides training in manual skill, resourcefulness and ingenuity. These qualities are quite useful for life.

A *word of caution* for teacher in using house-made apparatus is that he must not sacrifice efficiency just for his over enthusiasm for using house-made apparatus.

7.6 CHARTS, DIAGRAMS AND PICTURES

Charts, diagrams, pictures etc. if displayed in the laboratory provides right scientific atmosphere to the place various details about these have been discussed in chapter on *Teaching Aids*. Here the topic is discussed just as a reference.

Charts

An all out effort be made to avoid display of printed charts available in the market because these charts are quite costly and are not fully representative. Such charts are also sacrifice simplicity and directness to details.

Following type of charts be preferred for display in science room:

(*i*) Charts showing diagrammatic sketches of different pieces of apparatus generally used by students in their practical work. e.g. beaker, flask, gas-jar, retort, spirit lamp etc.

(*ii*) Charts depicting diagrammatic sketches of different important experiments from various branches of science e.g. chart showing the preparation of oxygen, hydrogen, carbon dioxide etc. Such a chart should be fully labelled and should be drawn in lead pencil.

(*iii*) Some charts for use in demonstration lessons e.g. a chart showing the working of a common pump or an air pump in stages, the chart showing charging of gold leaf electroscope by induction etc.

(*iv*) A progress chart depicting the progress of each student be prominently displayed. Such a chart should show the complete record of work of the student.

(*v*) Some important do's and don'ts be also displayed on a chart placed at some prominent place in the laboratory.

(*vi*) A chart of common accidents and first aid be also depicted in the laboratory.

In addition to various types of charts given above, the following types of *pictures* and *illustrations* are quite useful if depicted in the laboratory.

(*i*) Portraits of great Indian and world scientists.

(*ii*) Pictures of scientific interest e.g. pictures of Nangal Fertilizer Project, Picture of Bhabha Atomic Energy Centre etc.

(*iii*) Pictures showing progress of science, e.g. pictures of power stations, gas engines, aeroplanes, air-ships etc.

(*iv*) Maps indicating sources of ores of metals and chemical products.

(*v*) Weather charts, maps and graphs prepared by students after observing and collecting data from weather reports.

(*vi*) Variouas types of demonstration models preferably prepared by students.

7.7 BULLETIN BOARDS

Each laboratory is expected to have at least three boards to be used as bulletin boards. These are to be used as under

(*i*) One of the boards is reserved for display of newspaper cuttings, sciences news and pictorial illustrations of scientific interest.

(*ii*) One of the boards is reserved for putting up notices about science club activities.

(*iii*) One of the boards may be used for indicating the assignments.

7.8 IMPROVISED APPARATUS

For teaching of science availability of good apparatus and well equipped laboratories is a must. However it should lead us to a wrong conception that teaching of science cannot be carried out in the absence of expensive apparatus. One of the reports by NCERT observes that from among various factors that stand in the way of science education in our country one is lack of adequate resources for laboratory building, purchase of good and adequate apparatus and equipment. This lack of funds and resources makes improvisation of apparatus almost a necessity in India.

Need for Improvisation

India is a poor country and so we have only limited financial resources. For imparting effective and efficient science education, due to this financial constraint we require the production of improvised and inexpensive learning aids. A teacher with some ingenuity and manual skill can make a number of valuable and serviceable articles from discarded things all around him. For this purpose every since room should be equipped with a work bench and a kit of tools that may be used by students and teacher in making and improvising equipment for science teaching.

Definition of Improvisation

Some of the definitions of improvisations are given below:

It refers to a make shift arrangement for accomplishing the intended learning task.

It refers to contrived situation that is created from reading available material for sake of convenience.

It refers to a stimulating situation for demonstrating and imparting learning is respect of controls and operations making use of low cost materials.

It refers to those learning aids which are prepared from simple and readily available cheap material by students and teacher.

Significance of Improvisation

Improvisation is quite significant and has many values as the process of improvisation needs resourcefulness and ingenuity on the part of the science teacher. It is based on the concept of solving some problem by a make shift or alternate arrangement given below are some significant values attached with the process of improvisation:

(*i*) It splashes the cost of apparatus and is quite helpful in making the school self-reliant.

(*ii*) It has instructional value as well. When we are carrying out any improvisation we do get a proper feeling for the scientific process and designing. Thus we learn by doing.

(*iii*) It help develop the dignity of labour and also satisfies the urge of creative production.

(*iv*) It helps to develop the habit of cooperation and coordination.

(*v*) It provides training in thinking skills through the process of looking for low-cost substitutes or alternatives.

Process of Improvisation

It refers to a systematic way of constructing a piece of apparatus or designing an experiment. It involves the following steps:

(*i*) Making a careful study of the conventional apparatus or experiment.

(*ii*) Thinking of some low cost substitute that may be available in the market.

(*iii*) Designing the improvised apparatus or experiment.

(*iv*) Putting the improvised apparatus or experiment to test.

(*v*) Making further improvements in the improvised apparatus keeping the test results in mind.

(*vi*) Making use of the improvised apparatus in the laboratory for demonstration or practical work.

Examples of Improvisation

Physics Experiments

	Experiment	*Conventional apparatus parts*	*Improvised apparatus parts*
1.	Beam bending	(a) Steel strip (b) Spherometer (c) Slotted weights	(a) Wooden scale as beam (b) Wooden scale for depression measurements (c) Discarded cells and weights.
2.	Terminal velocity	(a) Glass tubes (b) Glycerin (c) Ball bearings (d) Iron stands	(a) Discarded fluorescent tubes (b) Water or oil (c) Sealing wax balls. (d) Mounting on the wall.

Following is the example of an improvised experiment.

Showing Self-inductions

To demonstrate self-induction we need a choke or primary coil of a step down transformer, a neon tester and a battery of 4 cells (6V dry cell battery) complete the circuit as shown in the diagram. When

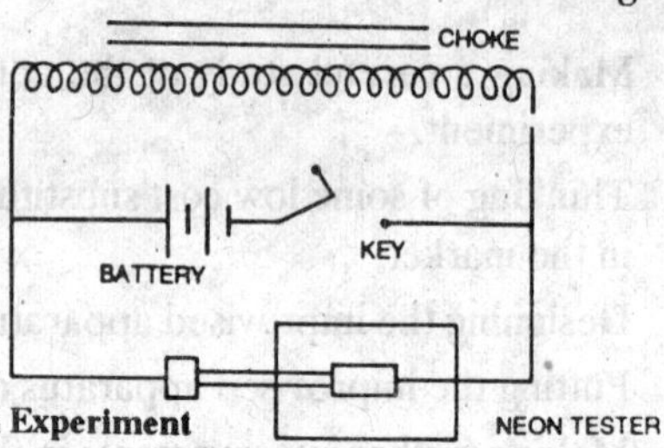

Fig. 7.3. Self-induction Experiment

we tap the key flashes can be observed by neon tester which show flashes. This is because of production of high induced e.m.f. in the same inductive circuit every time the circuit is broken.

Examples of Improvised Apparatus

Some examples of improvised apparatus are given below:

1. *Simple Tripod Stand*

To make a simple tripod stand we have only to cut away or shaped pieces from the sides of a discarded tin can. We can remove the lid and bottom of the tin can completely or we can simply make holes in the bottom. If holes are made it also serves the purpose of wire gauze.

Fig. 7.4. Tripod stand (improvised)

2. *Gold Leaf Electroscope*

For obtaining an improvised gold leaf electroscope we can take a wide mouthed bottle and fix a waxed cork in its mouth. Insert an L-shaped brass or copper wire into the cork and attach the gold leaf at its end.

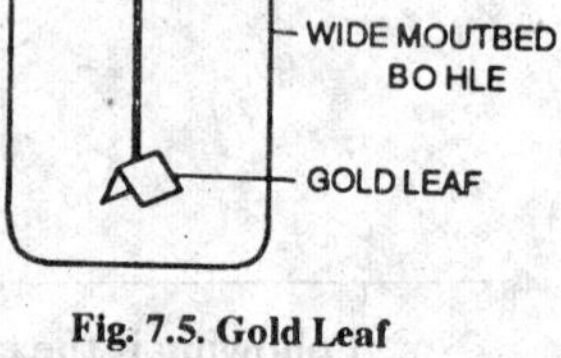

Fig. 7.5. Gold Leaf Electroscope (improvised)

3. *Davy's Safety Lamp*

To get a simple model of Davy's safety lamp we only need a wire gauze. Cut the wire gauze of the shape as shown and put it round a candle.

4. *Beehive Shelt*

An improvised beehive shelf can be obtained from empty tin can. The tin can to be used for the purpose should be rust free and its

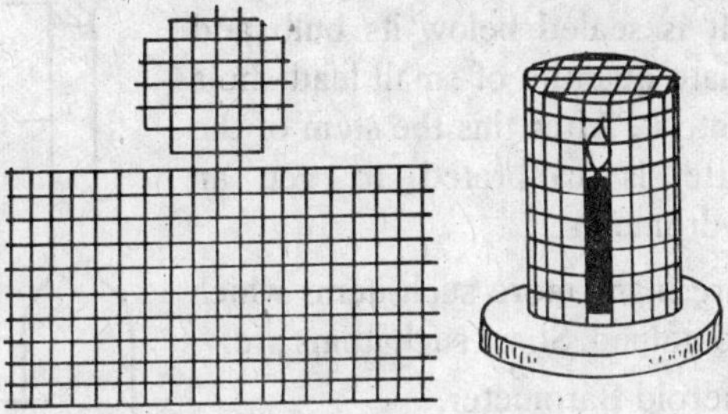

Fig. 7.6. Dany's Safety Lamp

inner and outer surfaces are either galvanised or varnished. To make a beehive shelf drill a hole of 1/2″ diameter in the centre of the bottom of tin can and cut a V-shaped notch on one side of it. This can now be used as a beehive shelf.

5. *Distillation Plant*

The design of a distillation plant is shown in Fig. 7.7.

In this boiling water from a kettle is allowed to condense in a jam jar which is immersed in a pan containing ice cold water. A simple glass tube fitted with a rubber tubing can be fitted to the mouth of the kettle and another glass tube is fitted to serve as outlet for condensed steam.

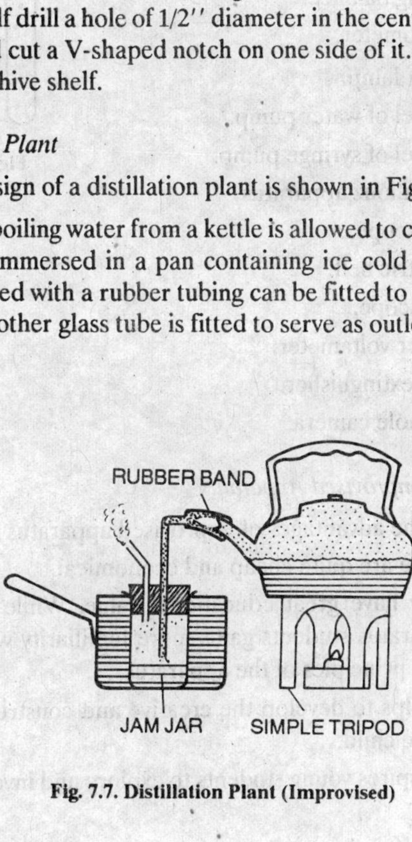

Fig. 7.7. Distillation Plant (Improvised)

6. *Hydrometer*

Broken pipettes can be used to prepare a hydrometer. It is sealed below its bulb and then appropriate quantity of small lead shots are inserted into it. After this the stem of the broken pipette is calibrated to get an improvised hydrometer.

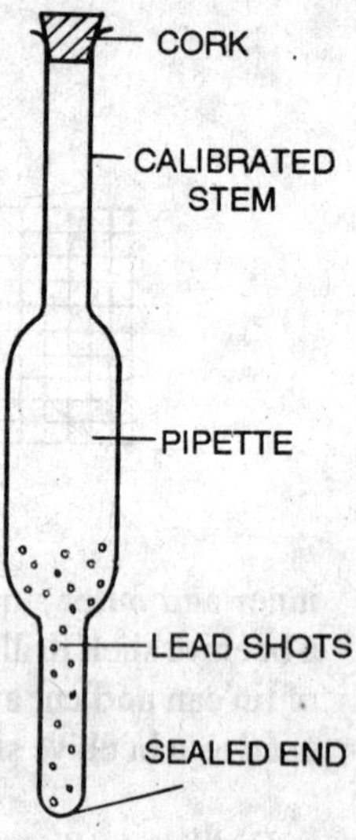

Fig. 7.8

There are many more such items which can be easily obtained. Some such items are.

(*i*) Aneroid Barometer.
(*ii*) Mariner's Compass.
(*iii*) Directing Needle.
(*iv*) Spring balance.
(*v*) Lactometer.
(*vi*) Spirit lamp.
(*vii*) Model of water pump.
(*viii*) Model of syringe pump.
(*ix*) Ingenhouz apparatus
(*x*) Telescope.
(*xi*) Electric bell.
(*xii*) Periscope.
(*xiii*) Water voltameter.
(*xiv*) Fire extinguisher.
(*xv*) Pin hole camera.

Advantages of Improvised Apparatus

Some of the advantages of improvised apparatus are

(*i*) These are quite cheap and economical.
(*ii*) They have great educational value. While devising such apparatus students gains more familiarity with the underlying principles of the apparatus.
(*iii*) It helps to develop the creative and constructive instructs of the child.
(*iv*) It inspires young students to explore and invent new things.

(*v*) It develops the lower of initiative and resourcefulness in the student.

(*vi*) It helps to develop power of scientific thinking.

(*vii*) It helps to inculcate the habit of diligency in the students.

(*viii*) It galvanises dignity of labour.

(*ix*) It solves problem of leisure time.

CHAPTER 8

The Science Teacher

8.1 INTRODUCTION

The success of failure of a science course rests mainly with the teacher. He may be provided with all the possible facilities in terms of laboratory, apparatus and equipment, given an ideal syllabus and a sufficient time for teaching of science but unless he is enthusiastic about his work, knows the subject and really knows how to teach science, he is not likely to achieve success. On the other hand a keen and well informed teacher who loves his subject and believes in its value will succeed inspite of difficulties and handicaps.

In this regard the Kothari Commission report (1966) says, "*of all the different factors which influence the quality of education and its contribution to national development, the quality, competence and character of teachers are undoubtedly the most significant*".

Dr. S. Radha Krishan emphasises the role of teacher in the following words, "*The teachers place in society is of vital importance. He acts as the pivot for transmission of intellectual traditions and technical skill from generation to generation, and helps to keep the lamp of civilisation burning. He not only guides the individual, but also, so to say, the destiny of nation. Teachers have therefore to realise their special responsibility to the society. On the other hand it is incumbent on the society to pay due regard to the teaching profession and to ensure that the teacher is kept above want and given the status which will command respect from his student.*

8.2 QUALIFICATION OF A SCIENCE TEACHER

A science teacher is expected to possess certain academic qualification as also certain professional qualifications.

As regards the academic qualifications it is usually a pass in matriculation/senior secondary examination for becoming a science teacher in a primary school. A pass in B.Sc. examination for being a science teacher in a middle or high school and a pass in M.Sc. examination in the respective subject for becoming a teacher to teach an elective science subject in a senior secondary school (grade 11 and 12).

In addition to the minimum academic qualifications any one who wish to be appointed a teacher in science has to undergo a teachers training course. For this purpose a person for appointment as a teacher in a primary school has to undergo 1 or 2 years Junior Basic Training (J.B.T) course and for appointment in high and higher secondary school the graduate or post-graduate teacher has to under a B.T. or B.Ed. course. This professional training is all the more important these days when new techniques of teaching, evaluation etc. are being introduced. Trained science teachers also require the stimulus of a refresher course to keep himself informed about the latest methods of teaching and to refresh his knowledge of science. Such a refresher course also provides him with an opportunity to see some of the latest books and apparatus concerning science teaching and to obtain instructions in arts and scientific hobbies. During such refresher course he also gets practical training in the organisation of science clubs, science fairs etc. For keeping himself in touch with latest in science the science teacher may visit some nearby schools where science is taught by new methods. He can also take up the membership of a good library or good science association. He can think of other such institutions and industrial houses nearby from where he can get the latest knowledge of science. All this is quite essential because a good teacher must always keep himself informed of the latest developments in the field. This aspect of a teacher has been brought out in the following words by Dr. Rabinder Nath Tagore, "*A teacher can never truly teach unless he is still learning himself. A lamp can not light another lamp unless it continues to burn its own flame*".

8.3 TIME ALLOTTED FOR SCIENCE TEACHING

We have already discussed it and given the allotment of time for science teaching in various countries. It can be conveniently assumed that about 100 hours are available in a year for teaching of science at elementary stage in India. This time should preferably be divided as under.

(*i*) Excursions, visits etc. 20 hours

(*ii*) Projects and allied activities 50 hours

(*iii*) Class room teaching 30 hours.

Generally two lessons of about half an hour per week should be sufficient at the primary stage.

At the middle stage three periods of 40-45 minutes per week should suffice. One of the three periods in a week be given to practicals and the remaining two to teaching.

At the high school stage an allotment of a minimum of three hours per week be made for teaching of science. Generally six periods of 40-45 minutes per week are allotted which includes laboratory work also. It would be more sound if an allotment of four periods for practical and two periods for theory is made. The four periods of practical work may be turned into two double periods of an hour and a half each.

If possible a free period be allowed to science teacher before his class so that he can prepare the experiment and the practical periods be so adjusted that they are just before the recess or in the last periods. Such an arrangement is useful because the teacher can allow some more time to the students to finish their practicals.

If instead of having two double periods for practical work, we have one double period and two single periods for this work and two single periods for class room work, the science teachers time table will be some thing like the one given below.

Days	*1st period*	*2nd period*	*6th period*		*8th period*	*9th period*
Mon.	Preparation	Demonst. X				Demnost. IX
Tue.	Preparation	Demonst. IX			Preparation	Demnost. X
Wed.	Preparation	Demonst. X		RECESS		
Thurs.	Preparation		Demonst. X			
Fri.					Practical IX	Practical IX
Sat.	Preparation	Demonst. IX			Practical X	Practical X

This is for a school having nine periods and providing a recess period after the 6th period.

8.4 SCIENCE TEACHER'S DIARY

Just like other teachers the science teacher should also keep a diary. In this diary the record of syllabus drawn up by science teacher be maintained. It should clearly indicate the particulars of quarterly and weekly distribution of work. A copy of the time-table be also kept in diary. The time table should clearly show the distribution of available time for (*i*) class room and laboratory work (*ii*) projects and other allied activities and (*iii*) out door activities (excusions, visits etc.).

A record of daily work be entered in the diary regularly and it should be dated. In keeping this daily record teacher should clearly mention the details of lecture-cum-demonstration work, individual experimental work, slides etc. to the shown and any such other details. He should also enter in his diary (*i*) those parts of the proposed work that have been accomplished (*ii*) those parts of the proposed work that could not be accomplished and (*iii*) any other extra work that has been attempted.

The diary should also show the details of written work, questions set. Entries of any comments on assignments and practical work must also find a place in teacher's diary.

If possible teacher should also mention the mistakes that were committed by a majority of students. Such an entry will be helpful to the teacher and he can explain these mistakes to the class.

The results of class tests and house examinations must also be recorded in teacher's diary. Science teacher can also keep a record of apparatus or chemicals to be ordered for his reference in his diary. Such a record will be quite useful for him when he is placing the orders at the beginning of the year.

8.5 STUDENT'S NOTE BOOKS

It is expected of each student to have three note books. One of these should be a practical note book, the remaining two are to be ordinary note books. One of these be used for taking notes and copying black board summaries and the other for assignments. It would be much convenient if all the students have same type of note books and the two note books to be used for taking notes and for assignment purposes are of different colours. Teacher should emphasise that all note books must be kept clean and maintained properly. It would be useful if right hand page is used for writing and left hand page is left blank for corrections, diagrams and calculations. This blank page can also be used for further notes from text books, library books, etc.

Record of individual practical work should be kept in the practical note book. The observation should always be directly recorded in fair practical note books.

For practical class some teachers use printed note books but such note books be avoided in high classes.

Note Taking

It is not possible even for a brilliant boy to take full notes of a lecture-cum-demonstration lesson during the class period. In class room the teacher say a good deal more than what a student can note down. Students fails to discriminate between essentials and non-essentials and it is only with a lot of practice and guidance of teacher that be learns to note down the important points of a lesson. The best way for taking down notes for the beginners is to copy the teacher's notes from the black board and then develop them at home. A record of the notes can be kept in any of the following two ways:

(*i*) The rough notes are taken down in the class and these are then noted down in a fair note book at home.

(*ii*) The notes are taken in a fair note book directly.

Both the above methods have some advantages. In the first method student will be able to write in fair note book neatly and would be able to draw neat and labelled diagrams. In second method the student acquires the habit of careful work and it also saves time.

Home Work

In science home work consists of preparatory part of assignment set, or of learning the work covered in a demonstration lesson or to write answers to one or two questions on the topic of demonstration. Occasionally keeping in view the availability of time teacher may ask his students to read from some popular science books, magazines etc. and even ask them to write some thing on them. A science student is also expected to keep a record, of individual experimental work done by him, in his practical note book.

Home work must be corrected and corrected properly by science teacher. The correcting and marking of note books take a lot of teachers free time but it is useless to assign work to students if the teacher does not find time to correct and mark their work. All efforts be made to reduce this work to a minimum. For this teacher may use some selected code of symbols to make corrections and ask the students to make corrections themselves.

While making correction all efforts be made by science teacher to point out mistakes in style and language. He should encourage the students to use a simple and straight forward language.

8.6 CO-OPERATION OF PUPILS OUT OF SCHOOL HOURS

Science teacher is required to take help of students during and even after school hours. During school hours be expects the help from students during a demonstrations-cum-lecture lesson. He seeks the help of students and asks them to read temperatures, light spirit lamps, hold a test tube etc.

Teacher can also take help from some sincere, brilliant and willing students who are keenly interested in science by assigning them work outside school hours. Such students may be asked to contribute to science museum, make some scientific models, charts etc. They can also be asked to clean science apparatus and arrangement of this apparatus in a proper way. Their help can also be sought to keep laboratory clean and tidy. Allotment of such work to students provides an excellent chance to a science teacher to channelise the energies of some naughty students. It also provides an opportunity to the teacher to assess the qualities of leadership and sense of responsibility in his students.

8.7 INSPECTION OF A SCIENCE DEPARTMENT

A regular inspection of science department is essential for its efficient running. A thorough inspection should be carried out at least once a year. The inspection be carried out by a team which must include at least one expert in science. While carrying out the inspection the inspection team should pay special attention to the following points.

(*i*) *Teacher.* The inspection team should see that the science teacher possesses the required academic and professional qualifications. The team should also pay attention to his teaching method. The individuality of teacher's method should be respected and the team if it so feels may suggest an alternative method but it should not be insisted upon. The inspection team should see that the science teacher practices proper correlation and coordination of science with other science subjects and also with other school subjects and environment.

(ii) *Scheme of Work.* Inspection team should see that the teacher prepares a quarterly and weekly scheme and such a scheme as shown in his diary is followed by him.

(iii) *Teacher's Diary.* The inspection team should see if the science teacher is maintaining his diary properly. Whether or not is he keeping a daily record of work done both in theory and practical, home work assigned etc. Has he noted down his time-table in diary? Is he having a good time-table? Is he having enough time for practicals? Is he teaching some other subjects? etc.

(iv) *Text Books and Library Books.* Are the students using approved and standard text books? What type of books are available in library? Are the students using library books?

(v) *Laboratory and Equipment.* The inspection team should see that adequate space and apparatus etc. are available in school. In the laboratory there is a provision for the proper storage of the apparatus, equipment, chemicals etc. Inspection team must make a report about the upkeep and tidyness of the laboratory. While making remarks about laboratory the following points be clearly mentioned.

(a) Were the pictures, charts, models etc. properly displayed in the laboratory?

(b) Did the arrangement exist in the laboratory for supply of water, disposal of waste water, first-aid box etc.?

(vi) *Stock Registers.* Maintainance of stock registers is one of the duties of science master and inspection team is expected to see that various stock registers are being maintained properly, accurately and regularly. It would not be improper if the inspection team carries out the physical verification of some items and find out for themselves if the actual stock agrees with the balance shown in the stock register. The checking of stock register includes the checking of requirements register and the preparation of indents etc.

(*vii*) *Class work and Home work of Students.* It can easily be seen from the note books maintained by the students. The inspection team should satisfy itself that the amount of written work done by the students is sufficient. Practical note books and assignments have been checked properly and regularly by the teacher and the mistakes have been pointed out to the students.

(*viii*) *Science Library and Science Museum.* The importance of science library and science museum for teaching of science is given elsewhere in the book. The inspection team write carrying out the inspection of science department in a school should find if a science library and science museum of some good standard exist in the school? Is the school library being used properly by the students? Are there arrangements for regular issue and return of books from science library? What method is used by science teacher to satisfy himself that his students regularly devote some time to the study of library books?

(*ix*) *Extra-curricular Activities.* The existence of a science club is a school provides an opportunity for carrying out extra-curricular activities. Inspection team should report, whether a science club exist? What are the activities of science club? How many tours excursions etc. have been arranged? How many of such excusions, tours were arranged to visit places of scientific interest? Has the school arranged any science fair during the year? How many films/ slides shows were arranged during the year? What steps were taken to encourage students to prepare home-made apparatus? Have the students contributed any good charts/ models during the year? Have any debate/declamation/ paper reading contest/quiz contest etc. arranged?

The inspection team should also ask for the record of all such activities carried out by the school during the year.

In addition to carrying out the inspection the inspection team is expected to give some constructive suggestions to the science master for all the activities for making improvements in science teaching in schools. Such suggestions should not be forced on science teacher and only those of these suggestions be implemented by the science teacher which are likely to bring about a qualitative, change in science teaching.

CHAPTER 9

Co-curricular Activities in Science

9.1 INTRODUCTION

For supplementing the teaching of science in class room and to widen the knowledge of his students a good science teacher can involve his students in a number of co-curricular activities such as the *science club, scientific hobbies, visits of places of scientific interest, broad-cast talks, gramophone lectures* etc. Though there is no limit to such extracurricular activities and teacher is free to undertake one or more such activities in his school for the benefit of his students.

Some of these activities, their organisational and other aspects, are taken up in the next few pages.

9.2 SCIENCE CLUB

To channelise the energies of students and to make proper use of talent of the students science clubs may be organised in schools. Such a club then forms the backbone of the co-curricular activities in the school. Such clubs, if properly organised, will be of great help to create interest in teaching of science and so now the importance and educational value of such clubs is duly recognised. Such clubs provide better chances to acquaint the students with various facts and principles of science. Students can take up any project or a scientific hobby of his choice while participating in a science club activity. Such a participation of a student in science club activities helps to link his theoretical knowledge to the outside world and he gets more opportunities for self-expression and creativity. Participation in various activities of science club also helps to develop manual skills of the student and he gets interested in learning of science.

The importance of science clubs in schools in words of Dr. W. Davis is, "*If the future belongs to youth and to science, then there is a vastly more important place for science clubs, in the scheme of things*".

Mckown has opined as follows while stating the advantages of science clubs over usual class room teaching.

"The club offers the pupil an opportunity for specialisation which he does not have in the class room. In the class room his work is formal; in the club it is informal; in the class room he is told what to do, in the club he chooses; in the class room his method of dealing with a topic is clearly outlined by teacher imposed restrictions, in the club programme the method is of his own desiring; in the class he tries to please the teacher, in the club he works for his own and his club's interest and for the joy of doing his works; in the class room he confirms to a system, in the club he suits his own convenience".

From the views expressed above we can clearly see that there is complete freedom for the students to pursue his interests in a science club and he can choose his own project and also his own method to pursue the project so chosen. This atmosphere that prevails in a science club is totally different from the one that prevails in a class room. The club represent freedom and expression where as the class room represents conformity and repression.

Types of Science Clubs

Broadly speaking science clubs can be classified as

(i) The Specialised Interest Science Clubs

In this catagory the clubs take up such projects which deal with some specialised subject. Such clubs are Radio club, photographic club, Nature study club, Aviation club, Astronomical club, etc.

(ii) General Science Club

These clubs take up any type of science activity and such clubs are generally known as chemical society, zoological society, Botony club, physics association etc.

Though both types of clubs have their advantages but experience has shown that specialised clubs are only short lived and so a science teacher should prefer general science club. He can undertake some specialised activity as a part of programme of such a general science club for a short duration of time.

Aims of Science Club

The major aims of science club can be summarised as under:

(*i*) To make proper use of leisure time.

(*ii*) To develop individual and group initiative.

(*iii*) To create students' interest in his every day experiences and his environment.

(*iv*) To develop scientific attitude among students and to inculcate a training in scientific methods and to broaden his scientific outlook.

(*v*) Provide the student with opportunity to develop his explorative, creative, and inventive faculties.

(*vi*) To develop a habit of cooperation in the students.

(*vii*) To encourage students participation in teaching-learning process.

(*viii*) To provide encouragement to club members for undertaking some difficult, complicated and even risky experiments which are not permitted to be undertaken in regular class.

(*ix*) To allow opportunities to young students to learn practical applications of science.

(*x*) To identify and nurture the would be scientists of the country.

(*xi*) To familiarise the students with recent advances in science.

(*xii*) To provide students vocational and educational guidance.

(*xiii*) To exchange information with other science clubs.

Organisation of a Science Club

A science club, if properly organised, will be a great help in enlivening the teaching of science. Such a club should be run by the students under the guidance and supervision of the teacher. For proper running of a club the most important thing is the preparation of a draft constitution of the club. This draft be prepared by the science teacher in consultation with the head of the institution. This draft constitution should provide all important details about the name of the club, aims and objectives of the club, details regarding membership and the fees etc. to be paid by members, purposes for which the expenditure can be incurred and the person competent to approve such an expenditure. Various offices available to members and the procedure for filling up such offices. Any other relevant details.

For efficient and successful working of science clubs an expert body has suggested the organisation as under:

(*i*) Such a club should have the head of institution as its pattern.

(*ii*) One of the senior science teachers be asked to be the sponsor of the club.

(*iii*) Membership of the club be open to all the science students of the school.

(*iv*) Associate-membership may be allowed to some other students interested in science.

(*v*) The club may have an elected executive committee. The members of executive should include the following and should be elected or nominated from amongst the students.

  (*a*) Chairman

  (*b*) Secretary

  (*c*) Asstt. Secretary.

  (*d*) Treasurer

  (*e*) One or two class representatives from each class.

  The executive committee may also include a librarian, a store keeper and a publicity officer.

(*vi*) Only a nominal membership fee be charged from the members.

(*vii*) The club members be asked to tap other resources and carry out the club activities in their own locality.

Assignment of Duties to Office Bearer of a Science Club

For a cohesive and efficient functioning of a club, there must be a clear demarcation of duties to be assigned to its office bearers. Following suggestions have been made in this regard.

Patron. He is expected to take a keen interest in all the activities of the club and to extend all the possible facilities to the club.

Sponsor. He is the main force to start the club and he has to take initiative to start such a club and made it a hub of activities. His role should be that of an advisor, guide and supervisor and he should refrain from becoming a dictator. He should always be alert to avoid any mishap. He should keep a strict watch on the activities of the club members.

Chairman. He being the elected representative of the student should be asked to preside over all the formal functions organised by the club. He has also the convene and preside over the meetings of the executive committee of the club.

Secretary. He is also an elected member and is to look after and maintain a proper record of various activities of the club. He should call a meeting of the executive committee in consultation with the chairman and in accordance with the constitution of the club. He should keep a true record of the meetings of the executive committee. He is also responsible to carry out all correspondence on behalf of the club and to extend invitations to speakers and guests for various functions of the club.

Asstt. Secretary. His main role is to assist the secretary in performance of his duties. In the absence of secretary he has to carry out all the functions of the secretary.

Treasurer. He is the person who is responsible for collection of subscriptions/membership fee for the club. He has also to maintain a proper account of receipts and expenditure of the club. He must present his accounts to the executive for audit and scrutiny at least once a year.

Members of Executive Committee. A member of executive committee is expected to extend his active cooperation and participate actively in formation of club's policy and programme. He should use his contacts and influence to make the programmes of the club a success.

Suggested Activities for a Science Club

(*i*) Interesting experiments may be undertaken in the club to enable students to develop skills and abilities for research work.

(*ii*) Club members may be asked to make collections of specimen, prepare charts and models etc.

(*iii*) Club can arrange excursions to places of scientific interest.

(*iv*) Science clubs may be asked to arrange science fairs and science exhibitions.

(*v*) Under the ages of the club some quiz contest, paper reading contest, essay competition and some such other competitions can be arranged.

(*vi*) Science clubs must celebrate science days. On such occassions they should put up tabuleaux and plays.

(*vii*) Some eminent scholars be invited to deliver extention lectures.

(*viii*) Science clubs can render school service in health and sanitation.

(*ix*) Members of the club can also render community service in realm of public health.

(*x*) If possible a science club should take initiative to organise a camp in which participants be educated to actively participate in national programme of health and family planning. They may be asked to inculcate sound health habits.

(*xi*) The club can take up the production of some common things like ink, soap, phenyl, shaving cream, boot polish, nail polish etc.

Science Club and Classroom Teaching

The activities of science club are a supplement to classroom teaching. Such clubs play an important role in making science education more meaningful and effective. Various charts, models, improvised apparatus prepared by members of the club can be used as important teaching aids for teaching of science in the classroom. References could be made to various science projects undertaken by the club members and the club members may be asked to explain their projects in the class. The explanation of a project by a student in a class may then be put to open discussion in the class which would make other students more interested in learning science.

To make best use of the trips and excursions arranged by the science club, the students be given a questionnaire so that students may be more attentive to provide their answers. Answers given by the students may then be discussed in the classroom and teacher can coordinate all the facts observed by the students into a complete lesson.

Some method can be used to correlate and coordinate various club activities with classroom teaching.

There is no doubt about the fact that if the club activities are organised properly they will never interfere with classroom teaching. Various activities of the club are expected to develop the skill of the student, his power of reasoning, understanding, his power to distinguish between relevant and irrelevant etc.

Evaluation of a Science Club

To find out the extent to which a club has succeeded in achieving its stated objectives it is necessary to carry out regular periodical evaluation of the activities of the club. Such an evaluation may be external or internal or it may be a mixture of both. For internal evaluation the views of patron, sponsor about the activities of the club may be obtained. They should express their views along with their suggestions for improvement in the working of the club. For external evaluation the sponsor of some other near by science club be asked to visit the club activities and express his opinion. He may also be asked to give suggestions for improvement. An effort be then made to further improve the working of the club in the light of suggestions given for improvement.

9.3 SCIENTIFIC HOBBIES

Scientific hobbies can also be undertaken as a part of activities of science club. Now that more and more attempts are being made to give a technical bias to our education and hobbies with a scientific basis are becoming more and more popular, the science master can make a valuable contribution by encouraging a number of hobbies that bear directly on education in science, students will be found only too enthusiastic and even willing to spend money in addition to their time to pursue such hobbies if the science teacher is keen and knows the particular hobbies he is going to start. In the beginning an attempt be made with one or two simple and less expensive hobbies. There is a large number of such hobbies having a scientific basis *e.g.* ink making, soap making, making hair oils and face creams, phenyl making, preparation of James and Jellys, achars and chutneys etc. The list can be enlarged to include gardening, making of charts and models, rendering first aid etc.

Uses of Hobbies Class

A hobbies class provides the student the best way of utilizing his leisure time and as such a hobbies class fulfills one of the chief aims of education *i.e. to train the child to use his leisure time properly.* The students get a good opportunity to keep himself busy in a constructive way by attending such hobby classes. It helps the students to keep himself away from adolescent disturbances that helps him to adjust in later years of life. Hobbies class also provide the student a knowledge of technical side of science and also helps in correlating the teaching of science with the every day life and environment of the student.

CHAPTER 10

Correlation in Science

10.1 INTRODUCTION

The major aim of education is the unification of knowledge existing in different branches of learning. To achieve such a unification a concious effort has to be made by teachers teaching various subjects. It is only by such a joint venture that we will be able to achieve the goal of unification of knowledge and bridge the gap that separates them.

10.2 IMPORTANCE OF CORRELATION

No subject can be taught in isolation particulary the subject known as '*science*. To take the learning process to its desired end we have to take full advantage of various correlations and applications of science. Just for our convenience we have divided science into different branches of study. However now we have fully understood the harm such a division has done to learning of science and now there is a concious effort to integrate various branches of science and to treat the subject as a synthetic whole. For this we have now devised such approaches as 'unit', 'topic' or 'project'.

10.3 TYPES OF CORRELATION

The three important types of correlations are:

(*i*) Correlation with daily life.

(*ii*) Correlation of various science subjects with one another.

(*iii*) Correlation with other subjects.

1. Correlation of Science with Daily Life (Environment)

Though the main of teaching science is to impart a training in scientific methods yet the study of science also aims to provide an insight into many of the natural phenomenon and also teaches us the various scientific principles that lie at the bottom of many simple rules of life. For fostering a love for science study among children teacher should bring home to his students the useful and interesting applications of principles of science in daily life. Every principle of science has some useful application in daily life and it is the duty of the teacher to emphasise these while teaching the principle. It is likely to make his lesson more interesting, stimulating and realistic. Teacher is free to include those phenomenon which are matters of every day experience even if these are not prescribed in the syllabus. Teacher should make a concious effort to arouse the interest of his students in such applications of science in every day life. Science teacher can find many applications of science in daily life and it would be much better if he quotes examples with rural background in rural schools and examples having urban background while teaching in urban background while teaching in urban school. For correlating science with every day life an effort be made to make use of available community resources. For example, a teacher can plan a visit to a power station or hydro-electric generator while teaching the generation of electric current. The topic on levers can be correlated with their functioning in human body and their use in agricultural implements etc.

Correlations of Science Subject with one another

It is not possible to divide study of science into water tight compartments of physics, chemistry, biology etc. because we find that there are many a principles and facts that are common to different science subjects. Because of this difficulty at present we find that subjects such as Bio-chemistry, Bio-physics, physical-chemistry, Geo-physics, general science etc. are emerging.

We can thus see that the science teacher can correlate his lesson in any one branch of science with some other branches of science using suitable examples. There are a plenty of topics which are common to two or more branches of science. For example.

1. *Atom and atomic structure*. It is quite common both in the study of chemistry and physics.
2. *Electrolysis and Electrochemical cells.* The study of these topics is also included both in physics and chemistry.
3. *Chemistry of life or living bodies.* It forms the subject-matter of both chemistry and biology.

4. Various topics in physics, chemistry and biology also help in the study of *Hygiene*. For example

Physics

During study of *light* in physics we can tell the students about the effects of light on health and can discuss the topics as light and germs; light and vitamins; artificial sun light; sun-bathing; Eye as camera etc.

The study of heat can be correlated to body temperature, heat and energy, humidity, treatment of heat burns etc.

While discussing a lesson on sound we can discuss the functioning of ear, effects of noise on health etc.

Similarly discussion of various other topics in physics can be suitably correlated with health and hygiene.

Chemistry

There a large number of topics in chemistry which actually revolve sound the chemistry of life. For example chemistry of cell, chemistry of food and digestive system, chemistry of blood and blood circulation, poisons etc. The effects of hard and soft water on our health. Ozone and importance of ozone layer etc. The effects of U.V. light. Fission of atom and atomic energy etc.

Biology

Biology is intimately connected with health and hygiene. In study of biology is included the study of development, structure and functions of body, breathing, circulation of blood, digestive system and various other systems of human body. It also includes the study of bacteria and the dependence of man on animals and plants.

In addition to relating the study of science to physics, chemistry, biology and hygiene it can also be correlated to other science subjects such as astronomy, geography, geology, home-science etc.

In the study of home science we find various topics which could be taught as applications of various branches of science. For example nutrition, laundry work, cleaning etc. are explained on the basis of knowledge of chemistry.

Correlation of Science with other Subjects

It is possible to correlate teaching of science with the study of almost any other subject. It can be correlated easily with mathematics.

(a) *Correlation with Mathematics*

Mathematics is considered as the mother of all sciences. A knowledge of mathematics is essential for understanding a topic in science. Science can be easily correlated with mathematics. The solution of practical problems, physical measurements, graphs of temperature, rainfall and pressure, laws of reflection, laws of refraction etc. all could be understand only with the help of knowledge of mathematics. In derivation of various equations in different branches of science an adequate knowledge of some fundamentals of mathematics is essential. Algebraic equations, graphs, geometry, calculus, coordinate geometry, statistics etc. are a few important branches of mathematics whose knowledge is used while teaching certain branches of science. The use of logarithms is gaining importance and science and mathematics teachers should cooperate and coordinate their teaching.

Mathematics and science teachers can supplement each other if the study of graphs in mathematics is illustrated by drawing graphs of some experimental data obtained by the students in a science practical class.

Similarly useful data for trignometry (a branch of mathematics) is provided by sextant (an instrument used to measure heights).

(b) *Correlation between Science and Geography*

The teaching of science can be easily correlated with geography. There are a number of topics which are common to science and geography. For example the study of rock and soils, study of plant and animal life etc. *Physical geography* requires an elementary knowledge of science for its foundation. For example principles of facts on which climate depends, instructions in use of a barometer, thermometer, sun-dial, magnetic needle etc. In all these fields such as the actual recording of atmospheric pressure, temperature, wind direction, rainfall etc. lies in the realm of geography but the study of recording instruments used forms the subject-matter of other branches of science. Geography interprets the results obtained by science. The study of various types of soil formed by weathering of different types of rocks is common to both science and geography. Not only in this but in various other topics the study of geography and science supplement each other. Of the various branches of science geology is quite akin to geography.

(c) *Correlation between Science and Art*

There is a close relationship between the study of science and study of art. In biology a student is required to draw a large number of diagrams which he cannot draw in the absence of a good deal of practice in art lessons. A large number of drawings are also found in physics and chemistry and for these also some practice in art of making drawings is essential.

Drawing and hand work are thus correlated to the study of science. Charts and diagrams for display in science laboratory should be good looking and quite durable. For this lettering should be done in script. Thus for drawing and lettering such charts the students needs the help of art.

The making models of scientific instruments, polishing articles of wood, soldering etc. can be encouraged among science students. In this way hand work can be easily correlated with the study of science. Such a correlation between science and work experience (SUPW) can be utilised in developing various improvised apparatus.

It is not only the science that needs the help of arts but arts also needs the help of science. A knowledge of chemistry of pigments, chemical properties of various types of dyes etc. is quite useful to art.

(d) *Correlation between Science and Music*

In science a student gets the knowledge of reasonance, reverberations, vibrating systems in strings and air columns, musical scales etc. which is quite useful to him to undergo the study of music. In music he comes across various types of instruments and equipments which are based on one or the other principle of science.

(e) *Correlation between Science and Social Studies*

There is a lot of correlation between science and social studies. Knowledge of science produces a great impact on our life style, way of thinking, our behaviour etc. A great change occurs in our outlook because of the influences of scientific knowledge. Science has revolutionised the civilisation. The advancement in technology and science have brought about a tremendous change in our social behaviour. The role of television, radio and other means of communication should be emphasised in the social science class and the science teacher should emphasise the fact there is only conceptual change in beliefs about God and life. In this way we find that a study of science can be easily correlated with the study of social science and vice-versa.

(f) *Correlation between Science and Language*

Science can be correlated to a language *e.g.* English. A science teacher also acts as an English teacher when he corrects the oral and written description of his students. While making such corrections he makes correction from scientific point of view as also from point of view of language. Not only English teacher but any language or composition teacher has to correct essays dealing with scientific topics. For a better correlation the language teacher may suggest essays on scientific topics and can also give passages for translation from historical scientific works. There are a lot of science books that deal with history of science, biographies of great scientists and important science works in various languages. All these are a valuable contribution to the literature in that particular language and are excellent and interesting reading material for the students.

(g) *Correlation between Science and History*

We can correlate important historical events with discoveries in science and in this way write a history of science. The history of science is very interesting. In the history of science we can find and correlate the fact of a certain discovery of science with the rule of certain kings. We can also mention the fact of some kings having patronised the teaching of science and some of the scientific discoveries can be attributed only to such a patronage. Some such personalities are the king of Syracuse and Archimedes, the king of Italy and Von Guericke.

A correlation exists between science and history can made more clear while discussing topics like the *story of earth, story of wheel, story of man's endeavours to fight* against diseases etc.

CHAPTER 11

Miscellaneous

11.1 SCIENCE KITS

With introduction of science as a compulsory subject in primary schools, the teaching of science posed a serious challange specially to remote single teacher village schools. To face this challange of teaching of science in such schools the idea of science kits originated. This is based on our age old belief that for teaching of science we need costly, sophisticated apparatus and equipment in addition to spacious and well built laboratories provided with all the essential amenities such as drainage, water supply and gas supply, since such facilities were not available in our village schools so the difficulties were faced even by dedicated science teachers in teaching of science in village schools.

With introduction of science as compulsory subject from class I to class X such facilities were required in more than 5 lakh primary schools, one lakh middle schools, 35 thousand high and higher secondary schools of the country. It was practically impossible to arrange the facilities for science teaching on such a large scale. This tremendous challange was met with by introducing and producing simple, inexpensive, improvised apparatus. Such apparatus is suitably stored in small handy boxes called *science kits*.

Unicef Aid for Project

Realising the importance of science teaching and introduction of science as a compulsory subject in India, UNICEF offered all out assistance to Government of India for achieving the aim of teaching of science as a compulsory subject and in upgrading the teaching of science in Indian Schools.

Utilising the UNESCO aid through NCERT, Government of India developed new curriculum for teaching of science in primary and middle classes and also devised science kits to cover the curriculum so developed.

To start with 50 primary and 30 middle schools were selected from each state to try out new curriculum and science kits. Most of the funds for translating new science books in various regional languages were provided by UNICEF. Funds were also provided by UNICEF to cover the cost of providing science kits to schools. In addition to these enough funds were provided, by UNICEF, for organising in service training of science teachers. For conduct of such inservice training of science teachers UNICEF provided funds to State Institutes of Science Education and Teachers training schools and colleges. These funds were used by such Institutes and colleges for the purchase of equipments, apparatus, work-shop tools and science kits required by them for the conduct of in service courses for science teachers. Thus we find that major financial burden for universal science education was born by UNESCO.

Science kits were prepared at Central Science Workshop (NCERT, Delhi) and some other production centres in our country. These are all UNICEF aided and so the whole process is known as UNICEF aided project.

Science Kit

Science kit contains quite simple, inexpensive, improvised apparatus which are stored in a small handy box. This box called *science kit* is simple in shops and is made of wood or iron and is provided with shelves and drawers. It can serve the function of a small movable mini-laboratory. Such kits are found to be very suitable for use in village schools where no facilities exist for science rooms or laboratories. Since the apparatus and equipment stored in such kits are indigenous. So these kits are quite cheap and the items can be easily operated: Majority of the items stored in the kit are quite hard and sturdy and thus there is no fear of these items getting broken so easily.

Separate kits have been developed for physics, chemistry and biology. Further separate kits have been developed for demonstration purposes (*Demonstration kits*) and for use in practicals by students (*Pupil's kits*).

Demonstration Kits

Demonstration kits contain such items which are needed by the science teacher for demonstration in class room. A demonstration kit has enough material for a class of about 40 students. The items stored in these kits are comparatively larger in size so that students sitting on back benches can distinctly see the various details of the apparatus, equipment.

Pupil's Kits

These kits contain sufficient items for various students experiments and one such kit can serve the requirements of a class of 40 students. In addition to apparatus these kits also contain consumable items such as chemicals etc. The store of such consumable items in a kit is expected to last one year.

The kits developed by NCERT are as under

1. *Primary Science Kit.* This kit can serve as a complete science laboratory for a primary school and can serve the purpose of a demonstration kit as of the pupil's kit.
2. *Physics Demonstration Kit No. I* } Both these are meant for class VI
3. *Physics Pupil's Kit No. I*
4. *Physics Demonstration Kit No. II* } Both these are meant for class VII
5. *Physics Pupil's Kit No. II*
6. *Physics Demonstration Kit No. III* } Both these are meant for class VIII
7. *Physics Pupils Kit No. III*
8. *Biology Demonstration Kit.* This kit is meant to cover various topics of biology (Science) for Class VI, VII and VIII.
9. *Chemistry Demonstration Kit* } These are meant for class VI, VII and VIII.
10. *Chemistry Pupil's Kit*

Contents of the Primary Science Kit

Primary Science Kit can serve the purpose of a demonstration kit as also of pupil's kit for classes III, IV and V. The kit box is made of iron and has provision for a chalk board and a demonstration table (collapsable). It is also provided with special shelf for hand tools which can be used for carrying out minor repair work if required.

Such a kit generally contains the following items.

1. *General Items.* General items such as Kerosene lamp, rubber balls, torch, thermometer, electric motor etc. are stored. Generally the total number of these items in a kit is about 50.
2. *Consumable Articles.* Consumable articles such as rubber bands, steel wire, rubber balloons etc. numbering about 15 are stored in a kit.
3. Some *chemicals* like sugar, washing soda and copper sulphate are also stored in a kit.
4. Kits are also provided with containers (3 in all) for chemicals.

Charts

Each kit contains a set of charts.

Hand Tools

Generally a set of 8 hand tools is provided in each kit. The hand tools include hammer, triangular files and pliers.

These kits are complete in themselves.

To make clear that these kits contains improvised apparatus let us consider some typical items stored in a kit.

1. *Kerosene Lamp*

It is made by using an ordinary ink phial. The stopper is made of ebonite and has three steps. The chimney has a large number of holes just as we have in house hold stoves.

2. *Spring Balance*

It is shown in Fig. 11.2. It has four graduations of 1/2 kg each and is a top pan type of balance.

3. *Water Pump Model*

It is used for demonstration and is made of a transparent polythene which allows the children to see the working of valves.

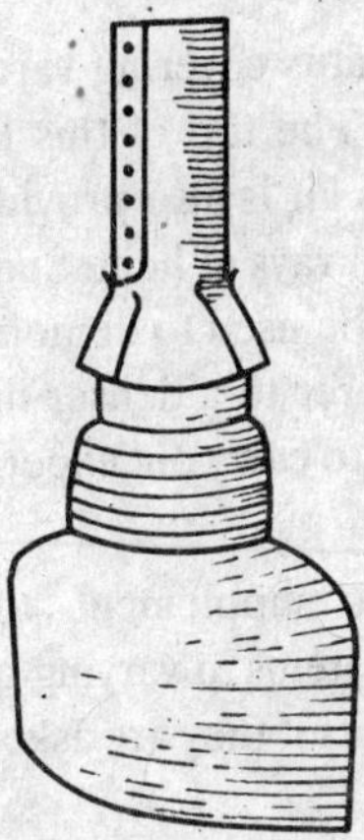

Fig. 11.1. Kerosene Lamp

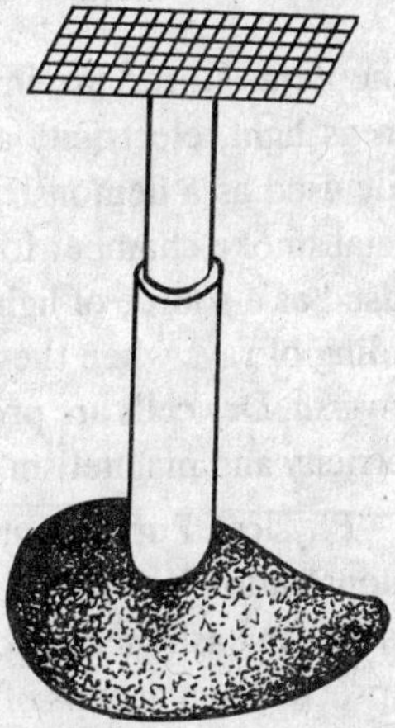

Fig. 11.2. Spring Balance

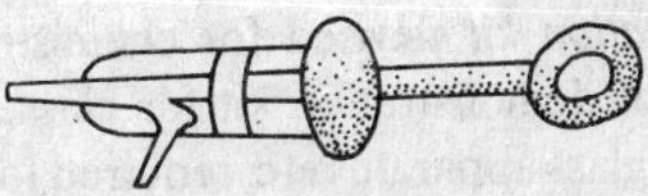

Fig. 11.3. Water Pump Model

Physics Kits

As already listed there are a total of six kits, for physics, devised by NCERT. Of the six kits three are demonstration kits and remaining three are pupil's kits.

Physics demonstration Kit No. I contains about 86 items arranged in a wooden box and covers the entire syllabus of class VI. These items are arranged in a number of trays in the wooden box.

Physics pupil's Kit No. I is for the use of students of class VI in their practical class and contains about 25 items. This kit can serve the needs of a class of about 40 students (two groups of 20 students each for practicals).

There are 71 items stored in physics demonstration Kit No. II which are arranged in four trays in a wooden box.

Physics pupil's Kit No. II contains 23 items (in multiples of 15) and is sufficient for providing each item to a group of 3 students. This kit can thus serve a class of 45 students.

Physics demonstration Kit No. III contains 74 items and can serve the purpose of demonstration kit for class VIII. In this kit most of the items stored are improvised apparatus covering various fields such as light, electricity and magnetism. The top of this kit can be easily used as a demonstration table. This kit is also provided with a special smoke chamber for experiments on rays of light. Sun light can be used as a source of light rays. This can be used to demonstrate the bending of rays when they enter from a rarer to a denser medium or *vice-versa*. Dry cells are provided in the kit to carry out experiments on electricity and magnetism.

Physics Pupils Kit No. III is a supplement to physics demonstration Kit No. III and contains 39 items in varying quantities. This kit can easily serve a class of 45 students if they are asked to carry out practicals in groups of three each.

Chemistry Kits

The *demonstration kit* devised for chemistry by NCERT can serve the purpose of demonstration kit for classes VII and VIII. It contains chemicals, glass apparatus etc. required for demonstration of various experiments. In it there is a total of 63 items of apparatus, 67 chemicals and it contains 12 types of containers. Apparatus stored in the kit is mostly improvised apparatus and the containers are bottles and ink phials. All the items of the kit are arranged in a suitable manner and are packed in a box made of wood. Such a box can be easily transported. This kit contains no liquid chemicals and these have to be arranged locally whenever the need arises.

Chemistry pupil's kit is meant for use of students in their practicals and it can serve as a 'mini laboratory' for village schools. The front covers of the kit can be hinged to serve as a table. It contains 37 different items, 40 chemicals and 10 types of containers for chemicals. It is also provided with two test tube stands, one on each side of the box. These can also be used as handles for lifting the box.

Biology Kit

This can serve as a complete biology laboratory for classes VI, VII and VIII. It contains 99 items for use by teacher for demonstration and for use by students in their practical classes. It covers the items from Plant life (botany), Animal life (zoology) and Human life (physiology). It also contains a set of hand tools which can be used by the teacher for carrying out minor repair work.

The kit opens on both sides and thus all the four sides can be used for demonstration. Zoology articles are stored on side I, side II and III store physiology items and side IV is used to store botanical articles.

For biology this kit also serves as the pupils kit and there is no separate pupils kit in biology.

Advantages of the Kits

Some of the important advantages of the science kits are summarised below:

1. *Low Cost.* These kits are very economical and a primary science kit costs only around rupees one hundred. All the kits for a middle school are not likely to cost more than Rs. 3000/-.
2. *Use of Indigenous Resources.* Majority of items stored in science kits are indigenous and no import or foreign collaboration is required.
3. *Easy Replacement of Items.* Various items stored in science kit can be easily replaced in case of loss or breakage etc.
4. *Easily Portable.* The kits are easily portable and can be easily used for demonstration in classes being met in open or under trees.
5. *Economy of Time.* Being planned in a very systematic way, minimum time is needed for setting up an experiment by using such kits.
6. *Consolidated Material.* All the essential items of apparatus, equipments, chemicals etc. are arranged in such a way that any item can be put to multipurpose use. In this way material is consolidated in a science kit. Moreover all the material needed for an experiment is consolidated in the kit.
7. *Economy in consumption.* In a science kit the items stored are in mini size and so the consumable items such as chemicals etc. are consumed in small amounts.
8. *Teacher's Innovation.* The science kits can serve to motivate and inspire an innovative science teacher to work out new ideas and he can encourage his students to improvise new apparatus and experiments.

9. *Students Involvement.* Since the various items stored in science kits are quite simple so they can be easily handled by the students. It encourages the students and they become active participants in the teaching-learning process.

Conclusion

The challange of imparting universal science education in various schools in India was boldly faced by Government of India. The role of NCERT must be commended as it devised very simple, economical and easy to operate improvised apparatus and suitably arranged and packed them in different boxes named science kits. These kits were found so handy and useful that we the science teachers shall ever be grateful to the NCERT for this innovation science kits have served their purpose so well that it is hoped that diversified efforts will be made by various science institutes and training colleges and schools in the country for furthur improvements and modifications in these science kits. These science kits are a boon to a science teacher and for proper appreciation and enjoyment of these kits science teachers are advised to make through study of kits and kit guides.

11.2 SCIENCE LIBRARY

One of the important recommendations made by the Secondary Education Commission was that every school should have subject libraries which are under the charge of subject teachers. It was felt that subject teachers can enrich their teaching making use of small collections of books on their own subjects. The need for subject library is utmost. A science library should be an essential part of each school which undertakes science teaching.

An explosion has occurred in scientific knowledge in the recent past the teachers find it difficult to keep themselves equipped with the newest knowledge in the subject. For acquainting himself with such a knowledge he needs a good science library where from he can find out at latest and new books to update his knowledge. He can then recommend some books to his students and may encourage them to acquire the habit of extending and supplementing their knowledge by making proper use of school library. Science library thus is a wonderful teaching-aid. By reading extra books students can get a good deal of general knowledge which he may not get if he depends entirely on the class room teaching.

Organisation

Though a well equipped subject library under the charge of subject teacher is desirable yet a *science library* under the charge of science teacher can serve the purpose of all science subjects. Such a library be set up preferably in a small room or in a corner of the science laboratory where some shelves or almirahs be reserved for storing the library books. The science teacher can equip the library depending on the availability of funds and accommodation for the purpose. For setting up a rich library with limited funds, it is necessary that science teacher is very thoroughly acquainted with the latest and good books available as the subject. For building up a good science liabrary teacher should select for the liabrary only such books which cover wide range of topics. These should be the books that deal with topics in physics, chemistry, biology, astronomy, geology, nature study, environment, ecology, pollution etc. Books on romance of science, engineering, scientific discoveries and inventions, science quiz, science projects, magic in science, experiments in science, fun in science etc. must also find a place in science library. Science library should also have some books on the lives and achievements of some great scientists and some books dealing with scientific hobbies like photography, motor cycle, radio, television etc. Some standard reference books and books on methods of teaching science be also purchased for school library.

The selection of books is a difficult task and science teachers can solve it by making use of fairly exhaustive list of science books available from various publishers. For list of such books he can also seek guidance and help from N.B.T. (National Book Trust) of India, NCERT and other such organisations as SCERT of their state. Science teacher should also read reviews of books published in some good journals for schools e.g. *School science review, popular science and industry etc.*

Recommendations of All India Seminar

Important recommendations about science library as made by All India seminar on the Teaching of Science are as under:

(*i*) Each school should have a separate science library.

(*ii*) Science books of general interest be stored in the school library.

(*iii*) A separate section be allocated in science library for reference books. Reference books are for use by teacher as also by students but these should not be ordinarily issued for home use.

(*iv*) Books on methods of teaching science be stored in a separate section in science library and these are meant for use of science teacher.

(*v*) Science teacher be asked to become in incharge of science library. He may be assisted in his library work by a small committee of students.

(*vi*) Teachers should take some measures to encourage love for library books amongst his students. Teacher can ask the students to prepare a brief review of the books read by them and some of these reviews considered good be published in science magazine and science bulletins.

(*vii*) A cross reference index be prepared in which teacher and students should indicate briefly the information contained in the book read by them. Such an information may be provided under the relevant heads and a proper use be made of this index for guiding the students in their reading.

(*viii*) Complete sets of various text books should be available in school library.

(*ix*) A few laboratory manuals must also be available in school library.

11.3 TEXT-BOOKS AND LABORATORY MANUALS

In the present educational set up the role of text-book is of prime importance. However we find that little attention is paid to this important aspect of education. Most of the text-books in science are not of good standard. They follow the prescribed syllabus too rigidly and no attention is paid to develop the topics according to the need and interest of students. A good text-book is one which is a source of knowledge arranged systematically and it enables the reader to acquire the needed information quickly. It inspires the student to invent, to discover and to inculcate scientific methods. However teacher should not depend solely even on the best of the text-books because even such a text-book omits many details which teacher wants to tell to his students.

The use of a text-book is made by the students for completing the preparatory part of an assignment. They also use their text-book for doing revision of course. Some students also consult and use their text-books to study at home, the demonstration lesson given to them by their teacher in school. In this way text-books are used to supplement the class work. Text-books also provide a help to students in correct understanding of basic concepts and principles of science.

Generally a number of books are prescribed by board or university to be used as text books. NCERT prepared text books are available upto class XII. While recommending a text-book to his students the teacher should consider the following points to assess the worth of the book.

(*i*) Correctness of matter.
(*ii*) Purity of languages.
(*iii*) Simplicity of diagrams.
(*iv*) Quality of printing and binding.

(*i*) *Correctness of Matter*

In this correction the standing of the author and the reputation of publishers should be considered. The books written by well known author having a long teaching experience of teaching the subject and possessing requisite qualifications be recommended. It would be much appreciated if certain minimum qualifications and experience for authors is laid down by authorities.

(*ii*) *Purity of Language*

A text-book that presents the subject matter in a simple, clear and lucid language should be preferred. For text-book in a regional language, the scientific terminology should also be given in English with in brackets. In such books only standard terminology evolved by the Central Ministry of Education and State Governments should be used.

(*iii*) *Simplicity of diagrams*

Only simple and well labelled diagrams be given in text-books. Such diagrams are self explanatory and help the student in properly understanding the subject matter.

(*iv*) *Quality of Printing and Binding*

It is desirable that a text-book makes use of a good quality paper and the quality of printing, and type of letters in fine. It should be so bound that its binding is appealing to the student.

In addition to the above a good text-book is expected to select and arrange the subject-matter in a psychological sequence. The book should follow the aims of teaching science and should serve as a guide for demonstration lesson as also for individual experiments. Each chapter should start with a brief introduction and a summary of the subject matter be given at the end of the chapter. Some assignments should also be given at the end of each chapter and the assignments should cover such areas as applications to life situations, numerical questions, suggestions for experimental work and projects, objective type tests etc. Heading and sub-headings be given in bold type. A table of contents be provided at the beginning and a subject-index be provided at the end. Glossary of some important scientific terms be given at the end of the book.

Each text-book should be accompanied by a laboratory manual. However the use of laboratory manual, unless good, should be avoided. The printed laboratory manuals give too many details and thus the work becomes almost mechanical.

CHAPTER 12

Evaluation

12.1 INTRODUCTION

Once a teacher has a clear idea of what she will teach and how she will teach it, she is concerned with knowing to what extent children learn from her lessons. This chapter will deal with specific procedures for evaluating the effectiveness of science teaching-learning.

Evaluation is a continuous process which is an integral part of teaching. It is not merely a test at the end of a science lesson or unit. Instead, evaluation goes on constantly during lessons and units and is clearly related to the teacher's goal and points of view on science teaching.

Besides being a continuous experience, evaluation is cumulative. A cumulative science record should be kept for all children. If such a record is available then his science exposure can be quickly and easily seen.

The recent trends in learning and evaluation link them to behavioural objectives. According to behaviourist psychology learning is defined as a *change in the behaviour of an individual that can be described in terms of observable and measurable performance*. The changes in behaviour are affected by providing experiences and through teaching.

The test efficiency of teaching, to judge the progress of students and to discover their achievements and evaluate the whole school system, we require some sort of measuring tools. These tools are *tests* or *examinations*. Tests are essential to grade and rank pupils, however if evaluation is used merely to indicate areas of science to which children have been exposed or for classifying and categorizing students, a great value is lost. The same loss occurs if evaluation is interpreted only as arriving at numerical or alphabetical ratings for report cards. In this way much of the positive use of evaluation as a means of teaching and learning could be destroyed.

Effective instructional planning and evaluation of students performance have always stressed upon the statement of instructional objectives so that they are of great help to the student. According to Muller, an instructionally usable objective must state the intended outcome in terms of the terminal behaviour of students. Terminal behaviour here stands for the behaviour of students after the class-room instruction and evaluation can be made if the learning outcomes are carefully specified. By coupling continuous evaluation with immediate application of what has been learned, the teacher can provide for:

(*i*) The stimulation of students who learn rapidly to greater growth toward goals by application of advanced works.

(*ii*) The identification of specific weaknesses and difficulties in functional understanding (concepts, principles, generalization) and the needed reteaching of varied activities skills or problem solving abilities, and

(*iii*) The clarification, modification or complete alternation of the goals as needed for the unit.

Evaluation, teaching and learning are the three corners of the education system. *Evaluation* is concerned with finding out how far students have learned as a consequence of teaching. There are two kinds of evaluation depending upon whether the comparison of student is made with some absolute performance standard or with other students of a given group. These are known as *criterion referenced evaluation* and *norm referenced evaluation*.

Criterion-Referenced Evaluation

It assesses the students performance in terms of a specified performance standard or criterion without any mention of the performance levels of the other students of the group. This evaluation method is related to mastery and developmental tests.

Norm-Referenced Evaluation

It assesses the students performance relative to other students of the group. Students are awarded marks and relative ranks in this method of evaluation.

12.2 PURPOSE OF EVALUATION

Evaluation fulfills the following purposes:

(*i*) It assesses the extent of learning by students and gives them the feed-back about their performance.

(*ii*) It gives feed-back to the teacher about the learning gaps of the students. It also provides the teacher a feed-back about the quality of his class room instructions.

(*iii*) It provides the student an opportunity to show his worth.

(*iv*) It serves as a screening tool for selecting students for special purposes.

Our evaluation has another goal besides assisting the teacher in assessing and modifying her teaching procedures. This goal *self-evaluation* is not solely for the students. As teacher and students actively engage in all levels of a study such as initial planning, organizing and carrying out activities they can be guided in developing ability to evaluate themselves. Knowing the general and specific goals can aid the pupil in checking himself all along the way. This makes the learner an active participant in class room activities. It also places same of the responsibility on him for learning and assessing what and how much he has learned. Self guided evaluation stimulates healthy and realistic achievement goals. A logical first step self evaluations is setting up of realistic goals. These goals for science teaching in elementary schools are:

(*i*) *Functional understandings* such as concepts, principles, generalizations, and the facts needed.

(*ii*) *Problem solving skills* such as defining problems, proposing hypotheses and techniques necessary for the solution of the problems, observational techniques, discussion and interpretations skills.

(*iii*) *Scientific attitudes, interests and appreciation* such as open mindedness and humanity.

The easiest area to evaluate is functional understanding because a rich variety of tests are well known and are widely used in elementary schools. Before we proceed to actual discussion of these tests let us consider the criterion of a good examination and pre-requisites of a physical test.

12.3 CRITERIA OF A GOOD EXAMINATION

Though a variety of tests are available to test the functional understanding of the child but for true assessment of such aspects of growth as the elements of reflective thinking, scientific attitudes, resourcefulness, creativeness or such other objectives or interests we require more precise and accurate instruments of evaluation. According to most of the psychologists and educationalists the following are essential criteria of satisfactory evaluation.

1. *Validity.* Any good test should measure what it claims to measure.
2. *Reliability.* A good test is one that is reliable i.e. it gives same rating to a candidate even if he is examined by different examines and even at different times.
3. *Objectivity.* A test can be considered objective if the scoring of the test is not affected in any way by the examiner's personal judgment. Thus the opinion, bias or judgment of the examiner can have no influence on the results of an objective test.
4. *Comprehensiveness.* By comprehensiveness of a test we mean that it covers the whole or nearly the whole course content and the questions are uniformly distributed to cover the course content.
5. *Practicability.* A test is called practicable if it can be easily administered and is acceptable to average examines. While preparing such a test, the time and cost of administration must be taken into consideration. The test should be usable and should serve a definite need in the situation in which it is used.
6. *Interpretibility.* A test can be considered as interpretable if its scores can be used and interpreted in terms of a common base having natural or accepted meaning.
7. *Easy to Administer.* A good test should be easy to administer so definite provision be made for collection and preparation of test material. It should give simple, clear and precise instructions.

Pre-requisites of a Good Test

There are certain pre-requisites for preparing a science test. These are as under.

Aspects	*Description*
Aims	– Acquisition of knowledge of various science concepts and skills.
	– Development of scientific attitude and interest.
	– Development of laboratory skills.
	– Highlighting the application of science in every day life and technology.
	– Development of skills of information processing, observation, enquiry and design
	– Acquisition of problem solving abilities.
Objectives	
(a) *Knowledge*:	Recall and recognition of factual information such as
	(*i*) definitions of various terms
	(*ii*) statement of laws, principles, rules, conventions etc.
	(*iii*) Description of construction and working of devices and instruments.
	(*iv*) Description of events, processes and phenomenon
	(*v*) Recognising the parts of devices, instruments, appliances and apparatus
	(*vi*) Identifying known physical phenomenon, events and occurrences.
(b) *Comprehension*:	Understanding facts, laws etc.
	(*i*) Company and contrasting various phenomenon
	(*ii*) Locating errors, limitations and defects.
	(*iii*) Illustrating scientific phenomenon.

Aspects	Description
	(*iv*) Reasoning events on the basis of scientific principles and laws.
(c) *Applications:*	Using knowledge in new situations.
	(*i*) Solving numerical problems
	(*ii*) Making use of various scientific laws in various situations and events.
	(*iii*) Relating various scientific variables.
(d) *Skills*:	Using psycho-motor skills.
	(*i*) Laying out an experimental set-up.
	(*ii*) Drawing diagrams, graphs, histograms, flow charts etc.
	(*iii*) Reading various measuring instruments.
(e) *Analysis:*	Breaking up information into parts to reach conclusions:
	(*i*) Interpretation observations
	(*ii*) Drawing inferences from observations.
	(*iii*) Generalising conclusions.
(f) *Synthesis:*	Combining parts of information to grasp a concept.
	(*i*) Designing an experiment
	(*ii*) Improvising and experiment, apparatus or device.
	(*iii*) Improving the accuracy of an instrument.

12.4 DESIGNING A SCIENCE TEST

A good science test should be constructed in accordance with a definite design or plan. The steps in designing a science test are as under.

(*i*) Allocation of marks for the different cognitive levels to be tested.

(*ii*) Allocation of marks for different chapters or units.

(*iii*) Blue print for the question paper.

(*iv*) Allocation of marks to various types of questions.

TABLE 12.1: Allocation of Marks for Abilities to be Tested

Ability	*Symbol*	*Marks*
Knowledge	K	45
Comprehension	C	26
Application	A	17
Skills	S	6
Analysis and synthesis	An/Sn	6
	Total	100

TABLE 12.2: Allocation of Marks of the Types of Questions

Question type	*Symbol*	*No. of questions*	*Marks*
Short Answers	SA	17	44
Structured	ST	4	56
	Total	21	100

Similarly allocation of marks for content areas is also made. For example in case of physics the content area wise split up of the marks is illustrated in Table 12.3.

TABLE 12.3: Allocation of Marks by Content Area

Content Area	*Marks*
Mechanics	38
Sound	11
Heat	12
Light	15
Electricity	24
Total	100

Finally on the basis of these allocations a blue-print of the questions paper is prepared. the blue-print on the basis of the allocations of marks in the above three tables is as follows.

TABLE 12.4: **Blue Print for Question Paper For the Test**

Content Area	*Abilities*									
	K		*C*		*A*		*S*		*An/Sn*	*Total*
	SA	*ST*	*SA*	*ST*	*SA*	*ST*	*SA*	*ST*	*ST*	
Mechanics	3	14	3	6	3	3	–	3	3	38
Sound	5	–	3	–	3	–	–	–	–	11
Heat	6	–	3	–	3	–	–	–	–	12
Light	3	5	–	5	–	2	–	–	–	15
Electricity	3	6	3	3	3	–	–	3	3	24
Total	20	25	12	14	12	5	–	6	6	100

After the blue-print is ready the actual question paper is set. Some of the commonly used tests in science are fill-ins, true-false, multiple-choice, short-answer or essay type etc.

Now we shall take up the discussion of some of these tests.

12.5 EVALUATION OF FUNCTIONAL SKILLS

Concepts, Generalization and Principles

The need of written tests becomes increasingly important as children progresses through the elementary school grades. This is so because of the following reasons.

(*i*) In upper grades pressures for more "objective evaluation" in science are greater as children are exposed to greater emphasis upon "subject matter grades".

(*ii*) As children's use of language increases, there can reasonably be greater emphasis upon meaningful written and verbal concept development.

(*iii*) As the child builds a background of science concepts, facts, understandings and inter-relationships, a greater need is presented for accurately assessing the child's knowledge.

(*iv*) With larger classes, as is generally the rule for the intermediate and upper grades, teachers require evaluation techniques that are fast, accurate, and easy to apply, score and interpret.

One of the types of written testing devices is the *short answer tests*. One major disadvantage is the superficiality and isolation of factual materials asked for rather than a breath and depth of understanding. They do however offer the teacher:

(*i*) opportunities for including wide ranges of items to be tested.

(*ii*) an ease of writing questions because of the shortness of each.

(*iii*) a minimum of time and effort is needed for scoring because of the shortness of answers expected, and

(*iv*) opportunities for involvement of pupils in the self-evaluation because of the ease of scoring and following up incorporate responses.

Basically there are two types of short answer testing devices recall and recognition examinations.

Recall Tests

As the term implies, recall questions ask the student to bring back to mind information that the student was exposed to in the past. Psychologists have indicated that the people usually associate items to be recalled with other items and information and rarely, if ever, completely isolate them. The way in which individuals associate isolated items is still much of a mystery. Even tests of isolation such as the inkblot design used in *Rorschach test*, evoke widely divergent responses because of unique back grounds and associations of individuals. Recall with children thus becomes a problem of framing questions in such a way as to stimulate the remembrance of the situation in which the intended information occurred. One of the ways in which this can be accomplished on recall tests is formulation of a question so that only one word or a few words in needed to answer the query. This simple question and answer procedure might look like this.

1. What is the approximate percentage of oxygen in air at sea level?
2. Name two organs of human body etc.

Another way of accomplishing recall of information in a science content study is by supplying statements with blanks to be filled in.

For example

1. ________ is provided for chicks to serve as teeth to grind their food.
2. The part of the plane that develops thrust that pulls the plane forward is the ________ .
3. Two by-products of the process of photosynthesis are ________ and ________ .

Recognition Tests

True and False tests are probably the most commonly used recognition tests in use today. The basic idea involved is illustrated below.

	True	False
1. Carbon dioxide is a product of photo-synthesis		
2. The crop of a bird is the bag filled with sand and gravel and mixed with digestive juices.		

Such tests encourage guessing and it greatly reduces the validity and reliability of the Tests. Because it is very difficult to frame questions that are neither too obvious nor too ambiguous, this type of examination should be used very sparingly. Whenever possible other types of recognition tests such as multiple choice test should be given.

Multiple Choice Test

In this type of test, several alternatives are presented to the pupil from which he must select the one that makes the statement most correct. Such test items can reduce the subjectivity in marking and inter-examiner variability in marking. These tests are the most popular these days and are most useful because in this way guessing is minimised and intelligent thinking is encouraged. Some examples of this type of tests are:

1. Honey bees gather pollen on their (a) wings (b) tongues (c) legs (d) none of these.
2. Mosquitoes lay their eggs (a) in food (b) in running water (c) on the blades of grass (d) in still water.
3. A scientist who studies rocks is called (a) a geographer (b) a geologist (c) a geometer (d) a geopolitist.

Reasoning power can play a big part in answering this type of questions and so called educated guesses should be encouraged. Actually these educated guesses usually are formulated from vague relationships that are seen or sensed. Very often the person cannot explain his reason for selection of correct choices in this type of questions, he just knows. Because there are so many aspects of learning and teaching that are still mysteries to us, teacher should not stand in the way of children learning. Intuition plays an important part in learning as well as in the scientific way of working.

Guidelines for Constructing Multiple Choice Test Items

While constructing multiple choice test items following guidelines be followed.

1. A test-item should have a single concept to be tested.
2. A test-item should be such that it can be used to discriminate a group of students as low, medium and high achievers.
3. The statement of test-item should be very clear and unambiguous.
4. Be sure that of the plausible answers only one answer is correct.

Parts of Multiple-Choice Item

There are generally two parts of a multiple choice test-item, viz., stem and plausible answers. The stem of the test-item contains the statement of the question or problem. There are some important styles of writing the stem of a multiple choice questions. These are:

1. stating the stem in the form of a question.

2. writing the stem as an incomplete statement.
3. writing the stem as a problem to be solved.

The plausible answers are the options available to the student from which he has to choose the correct answer. These are generally written according to following guide lines.

1. Write the answers in such a way that to a student who has not read the topic thoroughly each answer seems to be plausible.
2. Include common misconceptions which an average student holds about a particular learning segment.
3. Options which are true on their own but defy the statement of the problem given in the stem of the test item.
4. Do not provide clues for the right answers.

Cognitive Levels and Multiple Choice Items

Generally at the school level, the multiple choice questions in science are related to three cognitive levels, viz., knowledge, comprehension and application. Given below are a few examples of each kind of test items.

(a) *Knowledge Level Test Item*: We have generally noticed that the passengers in a moving bus fall forward when brakes are suddenly applied to it because of:

(a) Slippery seats
(b) Inertia of rest
(c) Inertia of motion
(d) Passengers being caught unawares.

(b) *Comprehension Level Test Item:* Choose the one in which no work is done.

(a) A car is moving up hill.
(b) A coolie is lifting the load up.
(c) An arrow is shot from a bow.
(d) A stone tied to a rope is whirled in a circle.

(c) *Application Level Test Item*: A car gets displaced by 4 m due east and then it gets displaced by 3 m due north. The vector substraction of these two displacements is –

(a) 5 m in W-N direction.

(b) 5 m in S-E direction.

(c) 5 m N-E direction.

(d) 1 m in N-E direction.

Limitation of Objective Type Tests

Some of the limitations of objective type tests are:

(*i*) They fail to test the ability to organise material.

(*ii*) They cannot test how well a thought is expressed.

(*iii*) They encourage guess work.

(*iv*) They are difficult to design.

Matching Tests

Besides the true and false and the multiple choice tests, there is a third type of recognition test, *the matching test*.

In this type of test items two mismatched columns are given, one working as problem statement and the other working as options. The questions and answers given in two columns are required to be matched or compared by the students. By giving the pupil two columns of items and asking him to match the related items, the teacher can quickly and easily see if his student recognises the relationships that exist between the items. There is less of a stress upon sheer memory or recall of fragmentary information because the materials are presented to the student for his correlation. Here are two columns of words that apply to the science study of our own bodies. Draw a line between the word on the right and the correct one on the left to show the proper relationship.

The word pelvis is correctly matched with the term trunk in the proper way.

	Pelvis
Head	Spine
	Knee joint
Legs	Breast bone
Trunk	Jaw bone
	Spinal Cord
Arms	Elbow joint
	Verbebrae
	Ribs
	Skull
	Collarbone

Because matching tests are focused mainly to measuring subject matter, it is not always indicative of the pupils ability to perceive the deeper meaning or real understanding of the relationship between the items used on the tests. Stress upon mere verbalization and memory of isolated bits of information should be avoided. Teachers will find it necessary to use all types of testing instruments so as to get a broad picture of the formulation of his children's science concepts.

Short Answer Tests

With all the drawbacks of the short answer tests, there is a wide use for these tests in science education for elementary schools. They are becoming quite popular these days. As the name suggests such questions expect brief, to the point, limited short answers. Generally the length of answers is specified. They offer the teacher an ease of construction and scoring not possible with other types of tests. The tests offer a greater degree of objectivity than other evaluating techniques and the results of tests can be helpful to the teacher for evaluating and reporting children's progress in science education to their parents. With the teacher's guidance, the simplicity of tests can be useful for self-evaluative examinations for the children. Children can also be involved in writing examinations of this type as well as in scoring them. Teachers can be assured that the objective tests being discussed warrant the expenditure of time and effort required to construct them in correct way. Correctly made, administered and interpreted, the short answer test offers many advantages to the teacher; however, they should never be used as sole testing device. They should only be used in conjunction with other types of oral and written tests as well as teacher observation.

Advantages of Short Answer Questions

Some of the important advantages of this type of questions are:

(*i*) They are easy to design

(*ii*) Scoring is less subjective and easy.

(*iii*) The question paper becomes comprehensive *i.e.* it covers the entire syllabus. The students lose the chance of spotting questions or topics.

Essay Tests

The essay-type examinations are in use in India since long and these have been greatly appreciated due to the freedom of response allowed. Essay tests aid in evaluating science understanding in the intermediate and upper grade of elementary school. Like all testing devices, essays present many serious disadvantages. At the same time they present many possibilities for gathering information. This type of test directs attention to and places emphasis on a larger segment of the subject or on an integrated total unit. It provides the student a chance to create a new approach to a problem as it requires the student to express his views in writing. He is required to produce some thing and not merely to guess or recognise the answer. These tests can measure verbal fluency, skill of expression, organisation of thoughts and the attitude of examinees towards problems and subjects considered in the class, however it lacks most of the qualities of a good measuring instrument.

Obvious advantages and disadvantages of essay test.

1. Shows how well the student is able to organise and present ideas,

   but

   scoring is very subjective due to a lack of set answers.
2. Varying degrees of correctness since there is not just a right or wrong answer,

   but

   scoring requires excessive time.
3. Tests ability to analayze problems using pertinent information and to arrive at generalization or conclusions,

   but

   Scoring in influenced by spelling, handwriting, sentence structure and other extraneous items.
4. Gets to deeper meanings and inter-relationships rather than isolated bits of factual materials,

   but

   Questions usually are ambiguous or too obvious.

Limitations of Essay Type Tests

These tests have low validity, low reliability and are less comprehensive. Discussing about the weaknesses of this type of tests Ross remarks, "The essay overrates the importance of knowing how to say a thing and under-rates the importance of having some thing to say".

This type of tests are not reliable because there is no agreement between teachers about the marks to be assigned and studies have shown that even the same teachers do not agree with themselves. Sandifoard, in his book on educational psychology refers to a study, "In one department of the University of Toronto, the same subject was set for an essay in different years. The essay which had secured 80 marks in one year, was exactly copied by the students in another year and scored 39 marks".

Ashburn who carried out a study at University of West Virginia concluded that, "the passing or failing of about 40% depends not on what they know or do not know, but on who reads the papers and that the passing or failing of about 10% depends on when the papers are read".

Another general complaint of students about essay type tests is that the questions 'did not suit them'. Certainly nine or ten questions generally set in this type of question paper cannot cover the whole syllabus. Hence this types of test is less comprehensive.

In an effort to offset the disadvantages the teacher must carefully consider the construction of each essay question. The teacher should word the question in such a fashion that the pupil will be limited to a certain degree to the concepts being tested. For example, it is better to use:

If you moved to Greenland, how would the days and nights differ from where you live now? How would the reason differ?

Than

Discuss the differences between the places in the world in relation to their days and nights throughout the reasons.

The second question is much too broad and does not give the pupil direction to know clearly enough what is expected?

To minimise the shortcomings of excessive subjectivity teacher should prepare a scoring guide before hand. Each question be scored separately and a list of important ideas that are expected should be made.

12.6 INSTRUMENTS FOR EVALUATING SCIENTIFIC ATTITUDES, APPRECIATION AND INTERESTS

One of the most important ways of judging the effectiveness of science teaching is to evaluate the growth of individual children. This is especially true in the areas of scientific attitudes, appreciations and interests. The most suitable techniques for obtaining this information are teacher observation and anecdotal records, tape recordings, rating scales, checklists, interviews, children's work products, essay tests and situation testing.

Teacher Observation and Record Keeping

Following forms have been found as useful aid by the teacher as it helps them in making their observations more accurate, systematic and time saving and also provides them with a permanent record of behaviour. These cards can be used for recording anecdotes of children's scientific or unscientific behaviour. As these records accumulate, the teacher can begin to see the direction of growth in behaviour and attitude. It is unsatisfactory to merely say that a child has improved in scientific thinking. We must have some records to substantiate our claims.

Tape Recordings

Use of tape recorder during science discussion period can be made for assessing the attitudes and interests of each student. Such tapes of discussions can be analysed by the teacher at his leisure. In many ways the tape recorded sessions have some important advantages over the written records of teachers observations. By use of tape records greater objectivity is possible. These tape recordings can also be used for self evaluation by students. It is expected that such tapes be used for science teaching and learning.

Checklists and Rating Scales

It is a faster but perhaps less comprehensive way of assessing growth in scientific attitudes and appreciations. A sheet is prepared by the teacher and she can use it for his own evaluation also and for modifying his teaching method.

Interviews

Personal interviews of individual or small groups of children enable the teacher to probe into their scientific attitudes and thinking. Interviews may last only a few mintues and the answers given by students are important primarily for the ways in which children attempt to answer and not the amount of factual material verbalised. A special session be organised for evaluation of skills in which practical situations are presented for assessing children's scientific thinking and attitude with greater elaboration.

Children's Work Products

Children's work in all aspects of the elementary curriculum provide us with much evidence about their scientific thinking and attitudes. Children's writings, particularly in the intermediate and upper grades, provide enough information about their concepts of the world and their thinking processes. Creative writing allows freedom for the child to explore scientifically and to speculate. Projects and reports provide the format for students to present examples of their thinking.

Situation Evaluation

The teacher can set up situations in which the student is required to find the answer to a practical problem. The student should be unable to supply the answer from memory because ideally he would never have encountered the particular situations. This procedure is quite valuable for assessing problem solving skills.

12.7 EVALUATING CHILDREN'S SCIENCE INTERESTS

For success of science teaching programme the children should strengthen and broaden their science interests through the evaluation process. Teacher can also analyse children's interest by their choice of books from the class, school or local library. An overview of science interests of children can be ascertained from their selection of reading materials. By keeping a record of reading interest inventories over a period of time, a teacher can see if children increase their voluntary selection of science books as a result of his science programme. The following types of reading inventories are popularly used.

Name
Book and Author
Dates read
Comments
Opinions

CHAPTER 13

National Talent Search in Science

13.1 INTRODUCTION

The discovery and development of the creative genius of our youth is of prime importance in educational process. It is precisely this ability that we must want to develop "catch them young" is a popular slogan. The secondary stage is considered right for identifying such talent.

The NCERT in collaboration with Directorates of education of various states initiated a programme for identifying promising students in science and to provide them with necessary help and encouragement to carry out their higher studies in basic and applied sciences under *Science Talent Search Scheme*. A pilot project was launched in 1963 in territory of Delhi and the scheme was extended to all over the country in 1964. Under the scheme about 350 scholars are selected each year. The scheme was previously open to students of science and mathematics but nor it has been thrown open even to students taking up social science subjects such as History, Geography, Political science, Economics etc.

13.2 NATIONAL TALENT SEARCH SCHEME

The Scheme

It basic aim is to identify outstanding students at the end of class X, XI and XII (where there is a public examination at the end of each class) and it provide them with financial aid for pursuing best possible education and help them to develop their talent for service of discipline as also of the nation.

The scheme is under the control of NCERT. However since 1985 the scheme has been decentralised and the State Councils of Educational Research and Training (SCERT's) are conducting the examinations. The students selected by the states are then finally screened by the examination conducted by NCERT and only those students who are finally selected by NCERT are awarded the scholarships.

13.3 OBJECTIVES OF THE SCHEME

The scheme aims to identify outstanding students at the close of the secondary stage. It also aims to stimulate scientific talent and help such students in pursuing their higher studies in basic and applied sciences. Scholarships are awarded from B.Sc. to Ph.D. level. Under the scheme some special programmes are provided in science so as to nurture the talent. The scheme also aims at encouraging schools to take an active interest in the search of talented students and in this way help in building up a body of scientists. Such persons (scientists) will then contribute in the scientific advancement of India.

The scheme is also expected to create a consciousness for improvement in science syllabi, methods of teaching science and evaluation techniques in science. It also hopes to provide colleges, universities and other technical institutions with a means of contacting science students of high ability. In this way it aims at mobilising the interest and support of higher education centres for development of science talent in the country.

13.4 SELECTION

For selection under the scheme the following procedure is followed.

(*i*) A written test is conducted to test general mental ability scholastic aptitude test is also given.

(*ii*) General mental ability test consists of test-items on reasoning, analysis, synthesis etc. Class X scholastic aptitude test contains items in Physics, Chemistry, Biology, Mathematics, History, Geography, Economics and Civics. The student has the the option to select any four of the light subjects noted above. Class XI and XII scholastic aptitude test has items in various subjects and a student has the option to select any three of the available subjects *i.e.* Physics, Chemistry, Biology, Mathematics, Statistics, History, Geography, Psychology, Economics, Political

Science, Sociology, Elements of Commerce and Accountancy. The student can offer English or any other Indian language as the medium of the test.

Those students who qualify the written test have to appear for an interview held at different places in the country.

13.5 ELIGIBILITY

The test in open to any regular student in Class X, XI and XII (at the end of which he takes a public examination). The blank forms for admission to the examination can be had from (i) Head of the Institution where student is enrolled (ii) Nearest Centre Superintendent of NTSE (iii) Field Advisor of NCERT (iv) Section Officer, NTSE Unit, NCERT, New Delhi.

Generally last date for submission of completed forms for the examination is 10th February. The completed form is to be submitted to the Superintendent of the Centre, at which the candidate wishes to take the examination.

Examination is normally held in May every year.

13.6 SCHOLARSHIP

Scholarships are given for studies at +2 stage and higher studies after suitable revalidation at terminal stages upto Ph.D. level in Basic and Social Science including Commerce and upto second degree level in Engineering and Medicines.

Continuance of Award

The continuance of award is subject to the maintainance of high academic standards (prescribed by NCERT from time to time). The scholarship available is subject to the following conditions

(*i*) The awardee must not fail in the class for which he is taking the NTSE or in any other subsequent class and must continue his studies as a regular student.

(*ii*) Scholarship is available for pursuance of higher studies in India upto degree level but is available for studies both in India and abroad for higher studies.

(*iii*) The payment of scholarship is made through the head of the institutions where the awardee is undergoing his studies.

Rates of Scholarship

The existing rates of scholarship are as under:

Name of Examination	*No. of Scholarships*		*Rates*
Class X	250	(i)	Rs. 150/- p.m. 2 years + Rs. 200/- p.a. for books
		(ii)	Rs. 200/- p.m. upto the second degree in Basic and Social Sciences and first degree in Engineering and Medicine + Rs. 300/- p.a. for books.
Class XI	100	(i)	Rs. 150/- p.m. for one year + Rs. 300/- p.a. for books.
		(ii)	Rs. 200/- p.m. upto second degree in Basic and Social Science and first degree in Engineering and Medicines + Rs. 300/- p.a. for books.
Class XII	150		Rs. 200/- p.m. upto second degree in Basic and Social Sciences and first degree in Engineering and Medicines + Rs. 300/- p.a. for books.

Appendix – I

Some Good Books for a Science Library

UNESCO Handbooks

1. The teaching of Science in Tropical Primary Schools.
2. The Training of Primary School Science Teacher.
3. The Teaching of General Science in Tropical Secondary Schools.
4. The Teaching of Chemistry in Tropical Secondary Schools.
5. The Teaching of Physics in Tropical Secondary Schools.
6. The Teaching of Biology in Tropical Secondary Schools.

British Council Books

7. Massey, N.B., Patterns for Teaching of Science, Macmillan.
8. Owen, C.B., Methods for science masters, Macmillan.
9. Saunders, H.N., the Teaching of General Science in Tropical Secondary Schools, Oxford University Press.
10. Savage, Sir, G., The Planning and Equipment of School Science Blocks, Murray.
11. Bryant, J.J., ed., Biology Teaching in Schools Involving Experiment or Demonstration with Animals or with Pupils, Association for Science Education.
12. Purvis, M.J. and others, Laboratory Techniques in Botany, Butterworth.
13. Guy, K., Laboratory Organization and Administration, Macmillan.
14. Newbury, N.F., The Teaching of Chemistry, Heinemann Educational.
15. Shaw, J.A., Chemistry Laboratory Management, Nelson.
16. OECD, Teaching Physics Today: Some important topics, 1965, Organisation for Economic Cooperation and Development.
17. Warren, J.W., The Teaching of Physics, 1966, Butterworth.

Appendix – II

Punjab University Chandigarh
B.Ed. Syllabus of
Teaching of Science for 1986 and onwards

I. Introductory:

1. Impact of Science and Technology on your modern living.
2. Aims and objectives of Teaching Sciences in the context of over-all educational and national goals, with special reference to scientific attitude and scientific methods.

II. Science Curriculum:

1. Place of Science in the school curriculum at the Primary, Middle and Secondary levels.
2. Principles of curriculum construction.
3. Planning at the Unit, and topic levels: the new objective based approach in lesson planning.
4. Critical study of the existing school science curriculum in any on class.

III. Methods of Teaching Science:

1. Traditional approach Vs. the New Problem-solving approach.
2. Inducive and Deductive Approach.
3. Specific methods of Teaching Science – Heuristic Method, Demonstration Method, Project Method, their comparative view.

IV. Instructional Material & Teaching Aids:

1. Science Text-book. Reference books and Science Journals.
2. Use of Teaching Aids.

V. Physical Facilities in Teaching Science:

1. Importance of Practical Work in Teaching Science.
2. Minimum Science Equipment and Apparatus for different types of Schools.

3. Need of Improvisation of Science Apparatus.
4. Science Kits and Mobile Laboratory.
5. Science Room and Science Laboratory.

VI. Evaluation

1. Examination Vs. Evaluation.
2. Tools of Evaluation.
3. Evaluation Theory and Practical in Science.

VII. Miscellaneous:

1. Special role of Science teacher in the School, his professional education and competency.
2. Science talent search.
3. Organisation of Science Club, Museum in the School and conducting various types of co-curricular activities pertaining to science (Excursions and trips, collection of materials for museum. Wall Magazine Contest, Organising Science Fair etc.).

Some Suggestions for Practical Work:

1. Content Orientation may be achieved through the preparation of detailed Lesson Plans during the Teaching Practice.
2. Training in Basic skills, such as weighing, measuring, cutting, bending, soldering, handling apparatus, and 10 usual equipment etc., may be given to all the teacher trainees.
3. Some items of improvised apparatus may be prepared by each teacher-trainee which may be preserved in the museum of the institution.
4. A Science Club may actually be organised in the college of education to conduct various science activities.
5. Preferably tours for teacher- trainees to places of Scientific Interest may be organised by the colleges of education.